THIS BOOK BELONGS TO

_____

START DATE

_____

SHE READS TRUTH

WHAT IS YOUR FAVORITE CHRISTMAS TRADITION?

EXECUTIVE

FOUNDER/CHIEF EXECUTIVE OFFICER
Raechel Myers

CO-FOUNDER/CHIEF CONTENT OFFICER ✱ *Stockings on Christmas morning*
Amanda Bible Williams

CHIEF OPERATING OFFICER
Ryan Myers

EXECUTIVE ASSISTANT
Sarah Andereck

EDITORIAL

EDITORIAL DIRECTOR
Jessica Lamb

MANAGING EDITOR ✱ *Looking for Christmas lights with cocoa and cookies*
Beth Joseph, MDiv

DIGITAL MANAGING EDITOR
Oghosa Iyamu, MDiv

ASSOCIATE EDITORS ✱ *Going to see a movie on Christmas Day*
Lindsey Jacobi, MDiv
Tameshia Williams, ThM

EDITORIAL ASSISTANT
Hannah Little

EDITORIAL INTERN
Bailey Shoemaker

CREATIVE

CREATIVE DIRECTOR
Jeremy Mitchell

LEAD DESIGNER
Kelsea Allen

DESIGNERS
Abbey Benson
Davis Camp DeLisi
Aimee Lindamood

JUNIOR DESIGNER ✱ *Rearranging the living room furniture to face the tree on Christmas morning*
Lauren Haag

MARKETING

CUSTOMER JOURNEY MARKETING MANAGER
Megan Gibbs

PRODUCT MARKETING MANAGER ✱ *Opening one gift on Christmas Eve (and it's always pajamas!)*
Wesley Chandler

SOCIAL MEDIA STRATEGIST
Taylor Krupp

LOGISTICS

LOGISTICS MANAGER
Lauren Gloyne

PROJECT ASSISTANT ✱ *Eating at a local hibachi grill after the Christmas Eve service*
Mary Beth Montgomery

COMMUNITY SUPPORT

COMMUNITY SUPPORT MANAGER
Kara Hewett

COMMUNITY SUPPORT SPECIALISTS ✱ *Extreme sledding on antique, steel runner sleds*
Elise Matson
Katy McKnight
Margot Williams

SHIPPING

FULFILLMENT LEAD
Abigail Achord

FULFILLMENT SPECIALISTS ✱ *Opening presents together and enjoying a homemade meal*
Cait Baggerman
Noe Sanchez

CONTRIBUTORS

PHOTOGRAPHY
Lauren Phariss (144)

RECIPES
Simoni Kigweba

SPECIAL THANKS
Tara-Leigh Cobble
Emma and Daniel Esquibel
Annie Glover
Jennifer Oatsvall
Julia Rogers

SHE READS TRUTH™

© 2021 by She Reads Truth, LLC

All rights reserved.

All photography used by permission.

ISBN 978-1-952670-35-0

1 2 3 4 5 6 7 8 9 10

No part of this publication may be reproduced, distributed, or transmitted in any form or by any means, including photocopying, recording, or other electronic or mechanical methods, without the prior written permission of She Reads Truth, LLC, except in the case of brief quotations embodied in critical reviews and certain other noncommercial uses permitted by copyright law.

All Scripture is taken from the Christian Standard Bible®. Copyright © 2020 by Holman Bible Publishers. Used by permission. Christian Standard Bible® and CSB® are federally registered trademarks of Holman Bible Publishers.

Research support provided by Logos Bible Software™. Learn more at logos.com.

Though the dates and locations in this book have been carefully researched, scholars disagree on the dating and locations of many biblical events.

ADVENT 2021

THE EVERLASTING LIGHT

SHE READS TRUTH

The centerpiece of this season
is always and only Jesus.

EDITOR'S LETTER

Amanda

Amanda Bible Williams
CO-FOUNDER & CHIEF
CONTENT OFFICER

I sat in the pews of the iconic Ryman Auditorium in Nashville, waiting for my friend Ellie to take the stage. It was an evening layered with reminders of God's faithfulness, weary souls filing into the stained-glass sanctuary to worship the God who never changes, even when the world turns upside down.

On my right sat Jonelle and her young daughter Emma, who'd come in from New York for the show. And though we'd never met, we immediately discovered we were far from strangers. A long-time reader with She Reads Truth, Jonelle described her affection for Scripture and the shelf in her home that displays the dozens of Study Books she's completed over the years. We marveled at a God so specifically kind that He would arrange for two women who've read the Bible together for nearly a decade to be seated side by side in a room that seated thousands. When I told her this year's Advent book would soon go to print, her face lit up with a knowing grin. "I can't wait for the reveal!"

There's a reason this season is so special. It's the time of year when we slow down and prepare our hearts for the celebration to come. We turn down the volume on the noise around us and return our attention to the God who rescues us. We read the first promises of the Savior in the Old Testament and watch expectantly as they are fulfilled in the New. We remember the weight of our spiritual darkness and train our eyes to look for the light.

This is our tenth Advent together as a community (can you believe it?!), and each one has come with its own circumstances, heartaches, and hopes. But the centerpiece of this season and this Study Book is always and only Jesus. He is in the Scripture we'll read, the questions we'll ponder, and the prayers we'll pray. We celebrate the joy of His birth with every delicious recipe and festive craft. Each chart, map, and hymn echoes the wonder of Immanuel, "God is with us." This five-week Advent experience is designed to testify to our hearts once again that Jesus is the embodiment of God's promise to bring light to a dark world. As we sing in the carol "O Little Town of Bethlehem": *Yet in thy dark streets shineth the everlasting light; The hopes and fears of all the years are met in Thee tonight.*

Friends, Raechel and I and our team are so thankful for you. Thank you for being women in the Word of God with us year after year, here in Nashville and around the world. We count it a privilege to read alongside you.

Merry Christmas!

✦

DESIGN ON PURPOSE

At She Reads Truth, we believe in pairing the inherently beautiful Word of God with the aesthetic beauty it deserves. Each of our resources is thoughtfully and artfully designed to highlight the beauty, goodness, and truth of Scripture in a way that reflects the themes of each curated reading plan.

For our Advent 2021 Study Book, we were influenced by Scandinavian design, known for its minimalistic aesthetic. This simplified approach sets aside clutter to focus on a few essential things. Our hope is that this design reflects an Advent season focused on what really matters.

The photography featured on our Grace Day spreads reflect the plan's theme of light. The visuals follow the reading sections, progressing from nighttime in week one to the sun rising as dawn approaches on the last Grace Day.

This book features lifestyle photography, with images of women practicing activities of both contemplation and celebration, rhythms that mark this season of anticipation.

MEET CHEF SIMONI

Simoni Kigweba hails from South Bend, Indiana, with roots in Burundi, Africa. He grew up with a love for cooking but started taking his passion seriously when he worked for a restaurant during college. Since then, Simoni has worked at many popular restaurants in Nashville, Tennessee, and now cooks full time as a private chef. Simoni has been a wonderful friend of She Reads Truth as he has prepared dinners for our team Christmas parties in years past!

Simoni lives and breathes the art of food and community. He often says, "all food tells a story." Whether it's where the ingredients come from, the creative vision for the meal, or the memories created around the table, he believes well-prepared food fosters narrative. Advent is a season of celebration, of actively remembering and enjoying the beauty, goodness, and truth that comes from our good God. We invite you to bring Chef Simoni's food to your table as part of your Advent celebration this year!

HOW TO USE THIS BOOK

She Reads Truth is a community of women dedicated to reading the Word of God every day.

In this **Advent 2021** reading plan, we will explore how Scripture presents Jesus as the embodiment of light in a dark world and invites us to live as people of light as we await His future return.

READ & REFLECT

Your **Advent 2021** Study Book focuses primarily on Scripture, with bonus resources to facilitate deeper engagement with God's Word.

SCRIPTURE READING

Designed to begin on November 28 (the first Sunday of Advent), this Study Book presents daily Scripture readings for the 2021 Advent season and through the last week of the year.

DAILY ADVENT REFLECTION

Each weekday features unique prompts for reflection and prayer.

COMMUNITY & CONVERSATION

The She Reads Truth community will start Day 1 of **Advent 2021** on Sunday, November 28, 2021. Join women from Indianapolis to Iceland as they read along with you.

 SHE READS TRUTH APP

Devotionals corresponding to each daily reading can be found in the **Advent 2021** reading plan on the She Reads Truth app. New devotionals will be published each weekday once the plan begins on Sunday, November 28, 2021. You can use the app to participate in community discussion, download free lock screens, and more.

GRACE DAY

Use Saturdays in this busy season to catch up on your reading, pray, and rest in the presence of the Lord.

SUNDAYS OF ADVENT

Each Sunday features a shorter Scripture passage as well as a prayer for the four Sundays of Advent and the two Sundays that follow.

EXTRAS

This book features additional tools and graphics to help you gain a deeper understanding of the text.

Find a complete list of extras on the following pages.

 SHEREADSTRUTH.COM

The **Advent 2021** reading plan and devotionals will also be available at SheReadsTruth.com as the community reads each day. Invite your family, friends, and neighbors to read along with you!

 SHE READS TRUTH PODCAST

Subscribe to the She Reads Truth podcast and join our founders and their guests each week as they talk about the beauty, goodness, and truth they find in Scripture.

Podcast episodes 104–108 for our **Advent 2021** *series release on Mondays, beginning November 29, 2021.*

TABLE OF CONTENTS

SECTION 1
The Light of the World

EXTRA	An Introduction to Advent 2021	14
EXTRA	The Seasons of the Church	18
DAY 1	A Prayer for the First Sunday of Advent	22
DAY 2	The Light of Life	25
CRAFT	Cross-Stitch Pattern	29
DAY 3	Let There Be Light	31
DAY 4	Choosing Darkness Over Light	34
EXTRA	Light in Scripture	38
DAY 5	The Father of Lights	42
DAY 6	A Light to All Nations	47
RECIPE	Golden Beet Salad	51
DAY 7	Grace Day	52
DAY 8	A Prayer for the Second Sunday of Advent	54
DAY 9	The Promise in the Stars	56
CRAFT	Beaded Tassel Garland	61
DAY 10	The Bright and Morning Star	62
EXTRA	The Genealogy of Jesus	66
DAY 11	The Consuming Fire	74
DAY 12	Light in the Darkness	78
HYMN	The First Noel	82
DAY 13	The Light of His Glory	84
RECIPE	Roasted Butternut Squash Soup	89
DAY 14	Grace Day	90
DAY 15	A Prayer for the Third Sunday of Advent	92
DAY 16	The Source of Light and Life	95

Never miss an update by scanning the QR code to add all things She Reads Truth Advent and more to your calendar!

GOLDEN
BEET
SALAD
PAGE 51

2

SECTION 2

People of the Light

DAY 17	Seeing the Light	100
HYMN	O Come, All Ye Faithful	104
DAY 18	Walking in the Light	106
DAY 19	Reflecting the Light	111
EXTRA	Prophecies of Jesus's Birth	114

3

SECTION 3

The Light Dawns

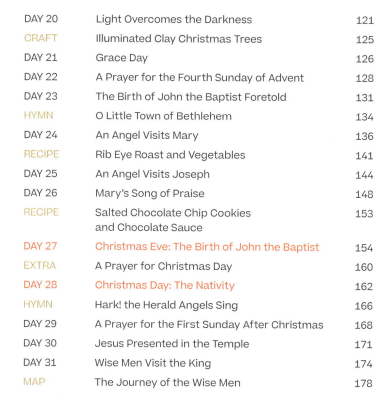

DAY 20	Light Overcomes the Darkness	121
CRAFT	Illuminated Clay Christmas Trees	125
DAY 21	Grace Day	126
DAY 22	A Prayer for the Fourth Sunday of Advent	128
DAY 23	The Birth of John the Baptist Foretold	131
HYMN	O Little Town of Bethlehem	134
DAY 24	An Angel Visits Mary	136
RECIPE	Rib Eye Roast and Vegetables	141
DAY 25	An Angel Visits Joseph	144
DAY 26	Mary's Song of Praise	148
RECIPE	Salted Chocolate Chip Cookies and Chocolate Sauce	153
DAY 27	Christmas Eve: The Birth of John the Baptist	154
EXTRA	A Prayer for Christmas Day	160
DAY 28	Christmas Day: The Nativity	162
HYMN	Hark! the Herald Angels Sing	166
DAY 29	A Prayer for the First Sunday After Christmas	168
DAY 30	Jesus Presented in the Temple	171
DAY 31	Wise Men Visit the King	174
MAP	The Journey of the Wise Men	178

ILLUMINATED CLAY CHRISTMAS TREES

PAGE 125

RIB EYE ROAST AND VEGETABLES
PAGE 141

4

SECTION 4

Waiting for the Light

DAY 32	The Second Advent	182
DAY 33	The Day Is Near	187
HYMN	O Come, O Come, Immanuel	190
DAY 34	The Everlasting Light	192
DAY 35	Grace Day	196
DAY 36	A Prayer for the Second Sunday After Christmas	198
EXTRA	For the Record	202

AN INTRODUCTION TO ADVENT 2021

Life Between Two Advents

"I am the light of the world. Anyone who follows me will never walk in the darkness but will have the light of life." JOHN 8:12

In this Advent 2021: The Everlasting Light reading plan, we will explore how Scripture presents Jesus as the embodiment of light in a dark world. This reading plan invites us to live as people of light as we celebrate His coming and await His future return.

Advent comes from a Latin word meaning "coming" or "arrival." As followers of Christ, we are a people living between two advents: the coming of Jesus as a baby in Bethlehem and His future triumphant return as the King of kings (Lk 2:11–15; Rv 21:5–7). During the Advent season, believers remember that Jesus Christ came as the Light of the World. We also remember the life Jesus was born to live, the salvation He brings, and the ongoing kingdom work He invites us to join.

Let's celebrate and contemplate this Advent season as people of the light, worshiping the living Savior and forever King who has come and who has promised to come again and dwell with us forever. This is the heart of Advent.

The people walking in darkness have seen a great light; a light has dawned on those living in the land of darkness.

ISAIAH 9:2

AN INTRODUCTION TO ADVENT 2021

Advent Rhythms

Since the fourth century, Christians have observed Advent to remember Jesus's birth and anticipate His return. What originally began as a season for believers to ready themselves for baptism grew into an annual season of **contemplation** and **celebration**. Use this Advent Study Book as a tool to practice rhythms that prepare you to celebrate Christ's birth on Christmas Day and prepare your heart for Christ's coming return.

A SEASON TO

Contemplate

This Advent season, contemplate your need for light in a dark world.

Contemplation is the practice of slowing down, repenting of sin, and resting in God's faithfulness.

This reading plan is designed to help you reflect on what it means to live in response to the first advent and in anticipation of the second. Make intentional time and space to sit in the presence of God. Pray, asking God to meet with you in the midst of a holiday season so full of distraction and to-do lists. Take time to slowly read through the daily Scripture, reflecting on the themes of each reading. End your time in God's Word with the daily questions, spending time in quiet prayer and anticipation. Reflect on the quotes and lyrics found throughout this book, inviting the words to enrich and ground you.

Celebrate

This Advent season, celebrate Christ's coming and rejoice in the promise of His return.

Celebration is the practice of actively remembering and enjoying God in our lives. The discipline of celebration cultivates joy as we acknowledge and rejoice in the beauty, goodness, and truth that comes from God.

Throughout this Study Book, you'll find opportunities to cultivate celebration. Sing the Christmas hymns aloud in joyful expectation and adoration. Cook the recipes and spend time with friends and family recounting how God has provided for you in the darkest of seasons. Read the Christmas traditions found throughout the book to discover how many favorite holiday practices are a reminder of Christ's arrival and future return.

The Seasons of the Church

The Advent season is just one part of the Church calendar, a centuries-old way many Christian denominations order the year to intentionally remember and celebrate the redeeming work of Christ. Structured around the moving date of Easter Sunday and the fixed date of Christmas, the liturgical Church calendar consists of six seasons as well as ordinary time.

EPIPHANY

WHAT IS IT?
Epiphany comes from a Greek word that means "to manifest" or "to show." It is also known as the Feast of the Three Kings, Three Kings' Day, and Twelfth Night. Epiphany commemorates the arrival of the wise men and is a reminder that Christ's birth is good news for all creation.

WHEN IS IT?
January 6, twelve days after Christmas. Some traditions celebrate this as a season through the Sunday before Ash Wednesday, rather than as just one day.

KEY SCRIPTURE
Mt 2:1–12

CHRISTMASTIDE

WHAT IS IT?
A season celebrating the birth of Jesus.

WHEN IS IT?
December 25 through January 5, also known as the Twelve Days of Christmas and Yuletide.

KEY SCRIPTURES
Is 9:2–7; Mt 1:18–25; Lk 1:26–38; 2:1–20

ADVENT

WHAT IS IT?
A season of anticipating the celebration of Jesus's birth, while also anticipating Jesus's promised return. The term *advent* comes from a Latin word meaning "coming" or "arrival."

WHEN IS IT?
Four Sundays before Christmas Day through December 24.

LENT

WHAT IS IT?
A solemn season of self-reflection, repentance, and Scripture meditation as a means of preparing one's heart and mind to celebrate Easter.

WHEN IS IT?
Ash Wednesday through Holy Saturday, forty fasting days and six feasting Sundays.

KEY SCRIPTURE
Lk 4:1–13

EASTERTIDE

WHAT IS IT?
A celebration of Jesus Christ's resurrection, the central belief of the Christian faith. Eastertide is the culmination of Lent.

WHEN IS IT?
Easter Sunday through the day before Pentecost. At seven weeks, it is the longest formal season of the Church year.

KEY SCRIPTURES
Lk 24:1–12, 36–53; Jn 11:25–26

PENTECOST

WHAT IS IT?
A celebration of when the Holy Spirit descended on believers from all over the world who were gathered in Jerusalem. It marks the birth of the Christian Church.

WHEN IS IT?
The seventh Sunday after Easter.

KEY SCRIPTURE
Ac 2:1–41

ORDINARY TIME

Most of the Church calendar consists of ordinary time, the period between Pentecost and Advent, and Epiphany and Lent. Though the colors used to mark the other seasons of the liturgical year differ from tradition to tradition, ordinary time is always green.

SECTION

1

THE LIGHT OF THE WORLD

"I am the light of the world."

JOHN 8:12

Jesus declared Himself to be the Light of the World. Apart from Him, we live in darkness.

But this story of light didn't begin with the birth of a baby boy under a shining star in the city of Bethlehem. From creation to the incarnation to the coming eternal city, Scripture speaks of our God as light in a world prone to darkness. In the midst of the sin and sorrow of this world, His light is a reminder of His life-giving presence and His power over sin.

In this first section of the reading plan, we'll explore together the role of light in Scripture to better understand the gift of Jesus, reading how God used light to remind His people of His presence and His promises.

DAY 1

A PRAYER FOR

the First Sunday of Advent

In the beginning was the Word, and the Word was with God, and the Word was God. He was with God in the beginning. All things were created through him, and apart from him not one thing was created that has been created. In him was life, and that life was the light of men. That light shines in the darkness, and yet the darkness did not overcome it.

JOHN 1:1–5

Almighty God, give us grace to cast away the works of darkness, and put on the armor of light, now in the time of this mortal life in which Your Son Jesus Christ came to visit us in great humility; that in the last day, when He shall come again in His glorious majesty to judge both the living and the dead, we may rise to the life immortal; through Him who lives and reigns with You and the Holy Spirit, one God, now and for ever. Amen.

THE *BOOK OF COMMON PRAYER*

CHRISTMAS LIGHTS

Why do we decorate with Christmas lights?

In 1882 in New York City, Edward Johnson, a trusted friend of Thomas Edison, took the stringed lights Edison had recently invented and used them to adorn his Christmas tree. Previously, candles had been placed on evergreen Christmas trees and lit to represent light piercing the darkness with the arrival of Jesus. Johnson's idea offered a safer, less hazardous way to celebrate this tradition. At first, the public did not trust the idea of electrical lights on a tree. It wasn't until 1895, when President Grover Cleveland featured the first electrically lit Christmas tree in the White House, that more people began to make the switch.

Here and throughout the book are the stories behind familiar Christmas traditions.

The Light of Life

02

JOHN 8:12

Jesus spoke to them again:

"I am the light of the world.

Anyone who follows me will never walk in the darkness but will have the light of life."

JOHN 3:1–21

JESUS AND NICODEMUS

¹ There was a man from the Pharisees named Nicodemus, a ruler of the Jews. ² This man came to him at night and said, "Rabbi, we know that you are a teacher who has come from God, for no one could perform these signs you do unless God were with him."

³ Jesus replied, "Truly I tell you, unless someone is born again, he cannot see the kingdom of God."

⁴ "How can anyone be born when he is old?" Nicodemus asked him. "Can he enter his mother's womb a second time and be born?"

⁵ Jesus answered, "Truly I tell you, unless someone is born of water and the Spirit, he cannot enter the kingdom of God. ⁶ Whatever is born of the flesh is flesh, and whatever is born of the Spirit is spirit. ⁷ Do not be amazed that I told you that you must be born again. ⁸ The wind blows where it pleases, and you hear its sound, but you don't know where it comes from or where it is going. So it is with everyone born of the Spirit."

⁹ "How can these things be?" asked Nicodemus.

¹⁰ "Are you a teacher of Israel and don't know these things?" Jesus replied. ¹¹ "Truly I tell you, we speak what we know and we testify to what we have seen, but you

do not accept our testimony. ¹² If I have told you about earthly things and you don't believe, how will you believe if I tell you about heavenly things? ¹³ No one has ascended into heaven except the one who descended from heaven—the Son of Man.

¹⁴ "Just as Moses lifted up the snake in the wilderness, so the Son of Man must be lifted up, ¹⁵ so that everyone who believes in him may have eternal life. ¹⁶ For God loved the world in this way: He gave his one and only Son, so that everyone who believes in him will not perish but have eternal life. ¹⁷ For God did not send his Son into the world to condemn the world, but to save the world through him. ¹⁸ Anyone who believes in him is not condemned, but anyone who does not believe is already condemned, because he has not believed in the name of the one and only Son of God. ¹⁹ This is the judgment: The light has come into the world, and people loved darkness rather than the light because their deeds were evil. ²⁰ For everyone who does evil hates the light and avoids it, so that his deeds may not be exposed. ²¹ But anyone who lives by the truth comes to the light, so that his works may be shown to be accomplished by God."

Jesus said, "I am the light of the world." Write a prayer asking to better understand Jesus as the Light of the World this Advent season.

DAY 2   NOVEMBER 29, 2021

Cross-Stitch Pattern

TOTAL TIME
20–30 hours

DIFFICULTY
✹ ✹ ✹

In keeping with She Reads Truth tradition, here is a cross-stitch pattern to help you slow down and reflect throughout the Advent season! As you work on this craft, contemplate how light has come into the world. Once finished, display your cross-stitch as a visible reminder to celebrate.

WHAT YOU NEED

Size 14 oatmeal cross-stitch fabric

10-inch embroidery hoop

Scissors

Size 24 tapestry needle

DMC embroidery floss in red (817) and white

Cross-stitch pattern

Scan this QR code to view or download the cross-stitch pattern!

WHAT TO DO

TO BEGIN

Find the center of the pattern (marked) and the center of your fabric. This is where you'll begin stitching. Center the fabric in the embroidery hoop and secure.

Cut a piece of embroidery floss the length of your arm, separate out 2 of the 6 threads, then thread them through your needle. Set the remaining 4 threads aside to use as you need them, 2 at a time.

To begin stitching, bring the threaded needle up through the back of the fabric, leaving a tail of about 1 inch of floss behind the fabric. Stitch the next 3 or 4 stitches over the tail. Clip off the extra thread.

STITCHING

There are two methods. The first method is to work a row of half stitches ////, then work back \\\\ to complete the X's. Use this method for most stitching. The second method is to complete each X as you go. Use this method for vertical or complex rows of stitches.

The sign of a real cross-stitch pro is when all of the X's are crossed in the same direction (that is, the top thread of the X always slants in the same direction, either \ or /). If you're a beginner, don't worry about this little detail. But if you're up for the challenge, give it a try!

FINISHING

When you come to the end of a thread, or to change to a new color, use your needle to weave the thread through the last 5 or 6 stitches on the back side of your fabric. Clip the thread short so as not to leave a loose tail. Then start your next color or another thread of the same color with the next stitch, securing the tail as you did before.

When your project is complete, remove it from the hoop. Before you display your work, smooth it out and remove wrinkles by placing another cloth on top of the needlework and pressing lightly with a warm iron.

Display your finished creation in a frame or in the embroidery hoop you made it in!

Let There Be Light

03

GENESIS 1:1–5
THE CREATION

¹ In the beginning God created the heavens and the earth.

² Now the earth was formless and empty, darkness covered the surface of the watery depths, and the Spirit of God was hovering over the surface of the waters. ³ Then God said, "Let there be light," and there was light. ⁴ God saw that the light was good, and God separated the light from the darkness. ⁵ God called the light "day," and the darkness he called "night." There was an evening, and there was a morning: one day.

PSALM 104:1–4
GOD THE CREATOR

¹ My soul, bless the Lord!
Lord my God, you are very great;
you are clothed with majesty and splendor.
² He wraps himself in light as if it were a robe,
spreading out the sky like a canopy,
³ laying the beams of his palace
on the waters above,
making the clouds his chariot,
walking on the wings of the wind,
⁴ and making the winds his messengers,
flames of fire his servants.

JOHN 1:1–5, 9–10, 14

¹ In the beginning was the Word, and the Word was with God, and the Word was God. ² He was with God in the beginning. ³ All things were created through him, and apart from him not one thing was created that has been created. ⁴ In him was life, and that life was the light of men. ⁵ That light shines in the darkness, and yet the darkness did not overcome it.

…

⁹ The true light that gives light to everyone was coming into the world.

¹⁰ He was in the world, and the world was created through him, and yet the world did not recognize him.

…

¹⁴ The Word became flesh and dwelt among us. We observed his glory, the glory as the one and only Son from the Father, full of grace and truth.

COLOSSIANS 1:15–20
THE CENTRALITY OF CHRIST

¹⁵ He is the image of the invisible God,
the firstborn over all creation.
¹⁶ For everything was created by him,
in heaven and on earth,
the visible and the invisible,
whether thrones or dominions
or rulers or authorities—
all things have been created through him and for him.
¹⁷ He is before all things,
and by him all things hold together.

¹⁸ He is also the head of the body, the church;
he is the beginning,
the firstborn from the dead,
so that he might come to have
first place in everything.
¹⁹ For God was pleased to have
all his fullness dwell in him,
²⁰ and through him to reconcile
everything to himself,
whether things on earth or things in heaven,
by making peace
through his blood, shed on the cross.

1 JOHN 1:1–4

¹ What was from the beginning, what we have heard, what we have seen with our eyes, what we have observed and have touched with our hands, concerning the word of life— ² that life was revealed, and we have seen it and we testify and declare to you the eternal life that was with the Father and was revealed to us— ³ what we have seen and heard we also declare to you, so that you may also have fellowship with us; and indeed our fellowship is with the Father and with his Son, Jesus Christ. ⁴ We are writing these things so that our joy may be complete.

What does today's reading reveal about Jesus's role in creation?

Write a prayer of gratitude for how knowing Jesus changes the way you experience the world.

___

___

___

___

___

___

___

___

___

___

___

___

DAY 3   NOVEMBER 30, 2021

DAY 4

Choosing Darkness Over Light

ISAIAH 5:20

Woe to those who call evil good and good evil,
who substitute darkness for light and light for darkness,
who substitute bitter for sweet and sweet for bitter.

GENESIS 1:26–31

²⁶ Then God said, "Let us make man in our image, according to our likeness. They will rule the fish of the sea, the birds of the sky, the livestock, the whole earth, and the creatures that crawl on the earth."

²⁷ So God created man
in his own image;
he created him in the image of God;
he created them male and female.

²⁸ God blessed them, and God said to them, "Be fruitful, multiply, fill the earth, and subdue it. Rule the fish of the sea, the birds of the sky, and every creature that crawls on the earth." ²⁹ God also said, "Look, I have given you every seed-bearing plant on the surface of the entire earth and every tree whose fruit contains seed. This will be food for you, ³⁰ for all the wildlife of the earth, for every bird of the sky, and for every creature that crawls on the earth—everything having the breath of life in it—I have given every green plant for food." And it was so. ³¹ God saw all that he had made, and it was very good indeed. Evening came and then morning: the sixth day.

The Old Testament contains numerous prophecies about the birth of the Messiah. You'll notice this icon next to each prophecy or fulfillment of prophecy in this reading plan. Turn to the "Prophecies of Jesus's Birth" extra on page 114 for a full list.

FULFILLED IN CHRIST
Galatians 4:4

GENESIS 3:1–15

THE TEMPTATION AND THE FALL

¹ Now the serpent was the most cunning of all the wild animals that the Lord God had made. He said to the woman, "Did God really say, 'You can't eat from any tree in the garden'?"

² The woman said to the serpent, "We may eat the fruit from the trees in the garden. ³ But about the fruit of the tree in the middle of the garden, God said, 'You must not eat it or touch it, or you will die.'"

⁴ "No! You will certainly not die," the serpent said to the woman. ⁵ "In fact, God knows that when you eat it your eyes will be opened and you will be like God, knowing good and evil." ⁶ The woman saw that the tree was good for food and delightful to look at, and that it was desirable for obtaining wisdom. So she took some of its fruit and ate it; she also gave some to her husband, who was with her, and he ate it. ⁷ Then the eyes of both of them were opened, and they knew they were naked; so they sewed fig leaves together and made coverings for themselves.

SIN'S CONSEQUENCES

⁸ Then the man and his wife heard the sound of the Lord God walking in the garden at the time of the evening breeze, and they hid from the Lord God among the trees of the garden. ⁹ So the Lord God called out to the man and said to him, "Where are you?"

¹⁰ And he said, "I heard you in the garden, and I was afraid because I was naked, so I hid."

¹¹ Then he asked, "Who told you that you were naked? Did you eat from the tree that I commanded you not to eat from?"

¹² The man replied, "The woman you gave to be with me—she gave me some fruit from the tree, and I ate."

¹³ So the Lord God asked the woman, "What have you done?"

And the woman said, "The serpent deceived me, and I ate."

¹⁴ So the Lord God said to the serpent:

> Because you have done this,
> you are cursed more than any livestock
> and more than any wild animal.
> You will move on your belly
> and eat dust all the days of your life.
> ¹⁵ I will put hostility between you and the woman,
> and between your offspring and her offspring.
> He will strike your head,
> and you will strike his heel.

PSALM 139:11–12

¹¹ If I say, "Surely the darkness will hide me,
and the light around me will be night"—
¹² even the darkness is not dark to you.
The night shines like the day;
darkness and light are alike to you.

PROVERBS 4:19

But the way of the wicked is like the darkest gloom;
they don't know what makes them stumble.

1 TIMOTHY 1:15–17

¹⁵ This saying is trustworthy and deserving of full acceptance: "Christ Jesus came into the world to save sinners"—and I am the worst of them. ¹⁶ But I received mercy for this reason, so that in me, the worst of them, Christ Jesus might demonstrate his extraordinary patience as an example to those who would believe in him for eternal life. ¹⁷ Now to the King eternal, immortal, invisible, the only God, be honor and glory forever and ever. Amen.

In Genesis 3:1–15, what were the consequences of choosing sin over life? What promise is present in the passage?

Write a prayer confessing your need for light
and life in the darkness of sin.

_____

_____

_____

_____

_____

_____

_____

_____

_____

_____

_____

_____

DAY 4   DECEMBER 1, 2021

LIGHT
IN SCRIPTURE

The theme of light appears continually in Scripture, from the beginning in Genesis where God speaks light into existence to the final chapters of Revelation, where Jesus, the Lamb, is the light of the eternal city. Sometimes light appears as a physical element. Other times it is symbolic of a spiritual principle. Many times, it is characteristic of Jesus Himself. As we celebrate Jesus Christ as the true Light of the World this Advent, note the different ways light is used throughout the Old and New Testaments.

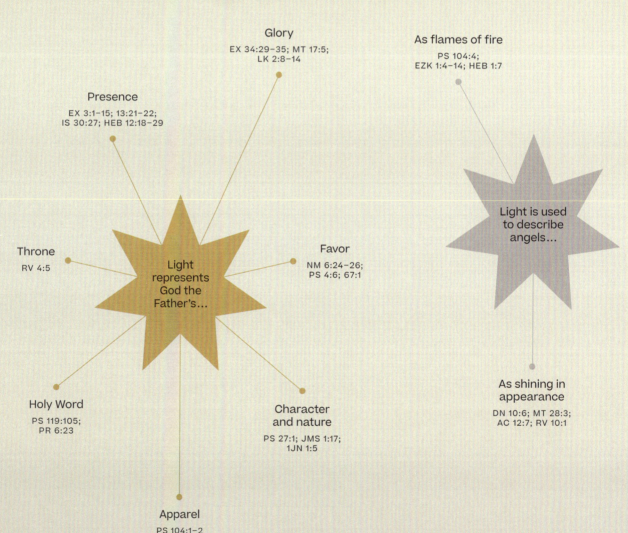

Light represents God the Father's…

Presence — EX 3:1–15; 13:21–22; IS 30:27; HEB 12:18–29

Glory — EX 34:29–35; MT 17:5; LK 2:8–14

Throne — RV 4:5

Favor — NM 6:24–26; PS 4:6; 67:1

Holy Word — PS 119:105; PR 6:23

Character and nature — PS 27:1; JMS 1:17; 1JN 1:5

Apparel — PS 104:1–2

Light is used to describe angels…

As flames of fire — PS 104:4; EZK 1:4–14; HEB 1:7

As shining in appearance — DN 10:6; MT 28:3; AC 12:7; RV 10:1

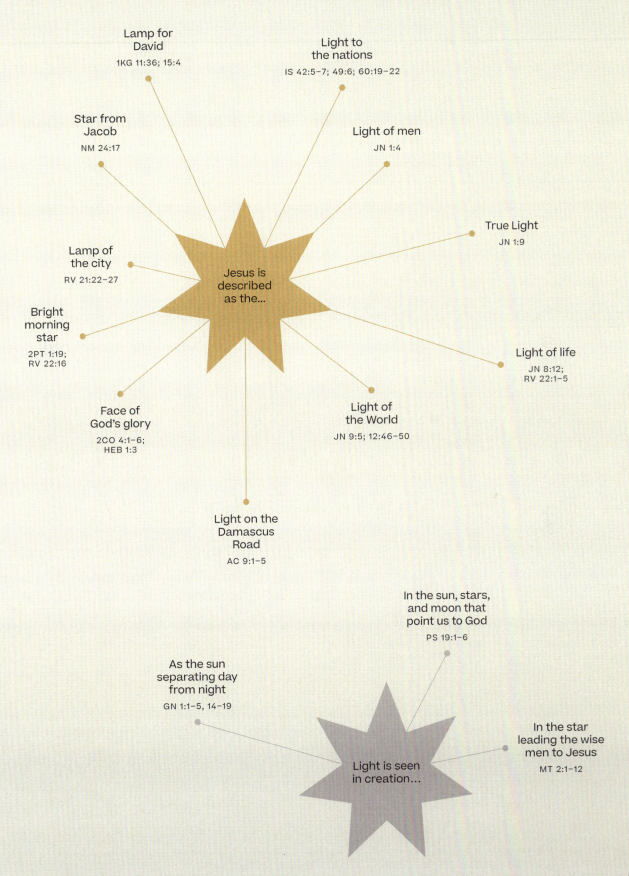

Believers are…

- **As numerous as stars in the sky**
  GN 15:1–6; 22:17–18

- **Light for the world**
  MT 5:14

- **Shining lights**
  DN 12:3; MT 5:16; PHP 2:15

- **Described as lampstands**
  RV 1:12–20

- **Children of light**
  JN 12:36; EPH 5:8; 1TH 5:4–5

- **Called into God's marvelous light**
  1PT 2:9

- **Rescued from the domain of darkness**
  COL 1:13

Believers are to…

- **Let their light shine**
  MT 5:16; LK 11:33–36

- **Walk in the light**
  JN 3:21; 12:35–36; 1JN 1:6–9

© 2021 She Reads Truth. All rights reserved.

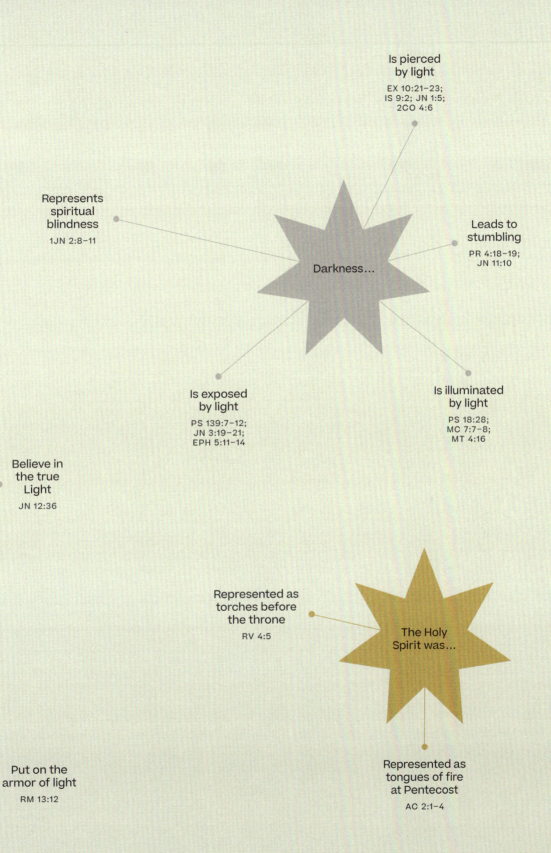

DAY 5

The Father of Lights

JAMES 1:16–18

ⁱ⁶ Don't be deceived, my dear brothers and sisters. ¹⁷ Every good and perfect gift is from above, coming down from the Father of lights, who does not change like shifting shadows. ¹⁸ By his own choice, he gave us birth by the word of truth so that we would be a kind of firstfruits of his creatures.

GENESIS 1:14–19

¹⁴ Then God said, "Let there be lights in the expanse of the sky to separate the day from the night. They will serve as signs for seasons and for days and years. ¹⁵ They will be lights in the expanse of the sky to provide light on the earth." And it was so. ¹⁶ God made the two great lights—the greater light to rule over the day and the lesser light to rule over the night—as well as the stars.

¹⁷ God placed them in the expanse of the sky to provide light on the earth, ¹⁸ to rule the day and the night, and to separate light from darkness. And God saw that it was good.

¹⁹ Evening came and then morning: the fourth day.

PSALM 136:1–9

¹ Give thanks to the LORD, for he is good.
   His faithful love endures forever.
² Give thanks to the God of gods.
   His faithful love endures forever.
³ Give thanks to the Lord of lords.
   His faithful love endures forever.
⁴ He alone does great wonders.
   His faithful love endures forever.
⁵ He made the heavens skillfully.
   His faithful love endures forever.
⁶ He spread the land on the waters.
   His faithful love endures forever.
⁷ He made the great lights:
   His faithful love endures forever.
⁸ the sun to rule by day,
   His faithful love endures forever.
⁹ the moon and stars to rule by night.
   His faithful love endures forever.

ISAIAH 59:1–2, 9–16

¹ Indeed, the LORD's arm is not too weak to save,
and his ear is not too deaf to hear.
² But your iniquities are separating you
from your God,
and your sins have hidden his face from you
so that he does not listen.

…

⁹ Therefore justice is far from us,
and righteousness does not reach us.
We hope for light, but there is darkness;
for brightness, but we live in the night.
¹⁰ We grope along a wall like the blind;
we grope like those without eyes.
We stumble at noon as though it were twilight;
we are like the dead among those who are healthy.
¹¹ We all growl like bears
and moan like doves.
We hope for justice, but there is none;
for salvation, but it is far from us.
¹² For our transgressions have multiplied before you,
and our sins testify against us.
For our transgressions are with us,
and we know our iniquities:
¹³ transgression and deception against the LORD,
turning away from following our God,
speaking oppression and revolt,
conceiving and uttering lying words from the heart.
¹⁴ Justice is turned back,
and righteousness stands far off.
For truth has stumbled in the public square,
and honesty cannot enter.
¹⁵ Truth is missing,
and whoever turns from evil is plundered.

The Lord saw that there was no justice,
and he was offended.
¹⁶ He saw that there was no man—
he was amazed that there was no one interceding;
so his own arm brought salvation,
and his own righteousness supported him.

JEREMIAH 31:35–37

³⁵ "This is what the Lord says:

The one who gives the sun for light by day,
the fixed order of moon and stars for light by night,
who stirs up the sea and makes its waves roar—
the Lord of Armies is his name:
³⁶ If this fixed order departs from before me—
   this is the Lord's declaration—
only then will Israel's descendants cease
to be a nation before me forever.

³⁷ "This is what the Lord says:

Only if the heavens above can be measured
and the foundations of the earth below explored,
will I reject all of Israel's descendants
because of all they have done—
   this is the Lord's declaration."

HEBREWS 13:8

Jesus Christ is the same yesterday, today, and forever.

What does today's reading teach you about the "Father of lights" (Jms 1:17)?

Write a prayer of praise for the good gifts
you've been given from God.

DAY 5 DECEMBER 2, 2021

CHRISTMAS TREES

Why do we bring evergreen trees inside and decorate them with ornaments?

The first Christmas trees were called "paradise trees." They represented humanity's fall in the garden of Eden. Traditionally brought into the home on Christmas Eve, these trees were decorated with apples, symbolizing the fruit Adam and Eve ate from the tree of knowledge of good and evil. Paper garlands, ribbons, nuts, round pastry wafers (symbolizing the communion wafer), and even candles were added to dress them up. Eventually, the apples were replaced with round bulb ornaments and the candles with the electric lights we're familiar with today.

A Light to All Nations

06

ISAIAH 42:5–9

⁵ This is what God, the Lord, says—
who created the heavens and stretched them out,
who spread out the earth and what comes from it,
who gives breath to the people on it
and spirit to those who walk on it—
⁶ "I am the Lord. I have called you
for a righteous purpose,
and I will hold you by your hand.
I will watch over you, and I will appoint you
to be a covenant for the people
and a light to the nations,
⁷ in order to open blind eyes,
to bring out prisoners from the dungeon,
and those sitting in darkness from the prison house.
⁸ I am the Lord. That is my name,
and I will not give my glory to another
or my praise to idols.
⁹ The past events have indeed happened.
Now I declare new events;
I announce them to you before they occur."

GENESIS 12:1–7

THE CALL OF ABRAM

¹ The Lord said to Abram:

Go from your land,
your relatives,
and your father's house
to the land that I will show you.
² I will make you into a great nation,
I will bless you,
I will make your name great,
and you will be a blessing.
³ I will bless those who bless you,
I will curse anyone who treats you with contempt,
and all the peoples on earth
will be blessed through you.

⁴ So Abram went, as the Lord had told him, and Lot went with him. Abram was seventy-five years old when he left Haran. ⁵ He took his wife, Sarai, his nephew Lot, all the possessions they had accumulated, and the people they had acquired in Haran, and they set out for the land of Canaan. When they came to the land of Canaan, ⁶ Abram passed through the land to the site of Shechem, at the oak of Moreh. (At that time the Canaanites were in the land.) ⁷ The Lord appeared to Abram and said, "To your offspring I will give this land." So he built an altar there to the Lord who had appeared to him.

ROMANS 4:13–25

THE PROMISE GRANTED THROUGH FAITH

¹³ For the promise to Abraham or to his descendants that he would inherit the world was not through the law, but through the righteousness that comes by faith. ¹⁴ If those who are of the law are heirs, faith is made empty and the promise nullified, ¹⁵ because the law produces wrath. And where there is no law, there is no transgression.

¹⁶ This is why the promise is by faith, so that it may be according to grace, to guarantee it to all the descendants— not only to the one who is of the law but also to the one

who is of Abraham's faith. He is the father of us all. ¹⁷ As it is written: I have made you the father of many nations—

in the presence of the God in whom he believed, the one who gives life to the dead and calls things into existence that do not exist.

¹⁸ He believed, hoping against hope, so that he became the father of many nations according to what had been spoken: So will your descendants be. ¹⁹ He did not weaken in faith when he considered his own body to be already dead (since he was about a hundred years old) and also the deadness of Sarah's womb. ²⁰ He did not waver in unbelief at God's promise but was strengthened in his faith and gave glory to God, ²¹ because he was fully convinced that what God had promised, he was also able to do. ²² Therefore, it was credited to him for righteousness. ²³ Now it was credited to him was not written for Abraham alone, ²⁴ but also for us. It will be credited to us who believe in him who raised Jesus our Lord from the dead. ²⁵ He was delivered up for our trespasses and raised for our justification.

GALATIANS 3:7–9

⁷ You know, then, that those who have faith, these are Abraham's sons. ⁸ Now the Scripture saw in advance that God would justify the Gentiles by faith and proclaimed the gospel ahead of time to Abraham, saying, All the nations will be blessed through you. ⁹ Consequently, those who have faith are blessed with Abraham, who had faith.

How was the promise of the Messiah good news for Abram in today's reading? How is it good news for you today?

Write a prayer of gratitude for Jesus,
the promised light for all people.

DAY 6

DECEMBER 3, 2021

Golden Beet Salad

PREP TIME
30 minutes

COOK TIME
1 hour

YIELDS
4–6 servings

DIFFICULTY
★ ★ ☆

A note from Chef Simoni:

Beets have a beautiful aroma and color during and after the roasting process. The key to this recipe is to use beets that are the size of a baseball or smaller. Uniformity will aid in the cooking process and preparation of the vegetable.

INGREDIENTS

BEETS

4 to 6 medium-sized golden beets

3 to 4 teaspoons balsamic vinegar

3 to 4 teaspoons olive oil

6 to 8 sprigs of thyme

1 tablespoon sea salt

1 tablespoon pepper

VINAIGRETTE

2 tablespoons honey

2 tablespoons dijon mustard

1 tablespoon lemon juice

1½ tablespoons red wine vinegar

1 tablespoon water

½ teaspoon salt

½ teaspoon pepper

1¼ cups grapeseed or canola oil

SALAD

1 large apple, diced

2 bunches of kale, cut into ¾-inch strips

3 stalks of celery, thinly sliced into half-moons

1 tablespoon extra virgin olive oil

1 tablespoon lemon juice

OPTIONAL GARNISH

Parmesan, grated

Breadcrumbs, toasted

Lemon wedges

Microgreens

METHOD

Set the oven to 400°F.

In a bowl, coat beets with balsamic vinegar, oil, thyme, salt, and pepper. Place beets in a deep baking dish lined with foil. Fill the bottom of the pan with a ½ inch of water. Roast beets for 1 hour, until tender or easily pierced with a small knife.

Meanwhile, using a food processor, or an immersion blender with a large plastic or glass container, mix the honey, mustard, lemon juice, red wine vinegar, water, salt, and pepper. Make sure the machine is running at a low speed and slowly add your grapeseed oil until the mixture has emulsified and looks creamy.

Peel skins using a kitchen towel. Cut each beet into 8 segments by quartering the beet and cutting those pieces in half. Set aside in a mixing bowl.

Salad can be mixed 15 to 20 minutes before dinner begins.

Mix the salad ingredients, sans the vinaigrette, in a large bowl. Add beets to the salad mixture, then two heaping tablespoons of vinaigrette and taste the salad. You should taste a balanced sweetness and acidity. Adjust the amount of the vinaigrette to taste.

Garnish with grated Parmesan, toasted breadcrumbs, or microgreens and serve with lemon wedges.

Grace Day

DAY 7

DECEMBER 4, 2021

Advent is a season of celebration and contemplation. We rejoice that our Savior has come to us! We also seek unhurried moments of quiet to reflect on His wondrous light and the promise of His future return. Take time today to pause from the busyness of the season to catch up on your reading, make space for prayer, and rest in God's presence.

DAY 8

A PRAYER FOR

the Second Sunday of Advent

We also have the prophetic word strongly confirmed, and you will do well to pay attention to it, as to a lamp shining in a dark place, until the day dawns and the morning star rises in your hearts.

2 PETER 1:19

DECEMBER 5, 2021

Precious Jesus, You are the Source, the Fountain, the Author, the Finisher of all.

Oh the depth of the riches both of the wisdom and knowledge of God! How unsearchable are Your judgments, and Your ways past finding out.

What was the day, the ever-blessed, ever-to-be-remembered day, when You—who commanded the light to shine out of darkness—shone in upon my heart?

And when did Jesus, the day-dawn and the day-star, arise to give us the light of the knowledge of the glory of the Lord, in the face of Jesus Christ?

Glorious light and life of my soul! Continue Your sweet influence, morning by morning, at dawn, and during the evening star of Your grace. Continue until, after many wintry days of my blindness, ignorance, and senseless state, You renew me in the precious discoveries of Your love.

By this I am carried through all the twilight of this poor and dying state of things below. For then I will awake to the full enjoyment of Your glory. I will see You in one full, open day; and I will be made like You in Your kingdom of light, and life, and happiness, forever and ever. Amen.

PRAYERS OF THE PURITANS

The Promise in the Stars

GENESIS 15:1–6

THE ABRAHAMIC COVENANT

¹ After these events, the word of the Lord came to Abram in a vision:

> Do not be afraid, Abram.
> I am your shield;

your reward will be very great.

² But Abram said, "Lord God, what can you give me, since I am childless and the heir of my house is Eliezer of Damascus?" ³ Abram continued, "Look, you have given me no offspring, so a slave born in my house will be my heir."

⁴ Now the word of the Lord came to him: "This one will not be your heir; instead, one who comes from your own body will be your heir." ⁵ He took him outside and said, "Look at the sky and count the stars, if you are able to count them." Then he said to him, "Your offspring will be that numerous."

⁶ Abram believed the Lord, and he credited it to him as righteousness.

FULFILLED IN CHRIST

Matthew 1:1–2

GENESIS 22:15–18

¹⁵ Then the angel of the Lord called to Abraham a second time from heaven ¹⁶ and said, "By myself I have sworn," this is the Lord's declaration: "Because you have done this thing and have not withheld your only son, ¹⁷ I will indeed bless you and make your offspring as numerous as the stars of the sky and the sand on the seashore. Your offspring will possess the city gates of their enemies. ¹⁸ And all the nations of the earth will be blessed by your offspring because you have obeyed my command."

JOB 9:7–10

⁷ He commands the sun not to shine
and seals off the stars.
⁸ He alone stretches out the heavens
and treads on the waves of the sea.
⁹ He makes the stars: the Bear, Orion,
the Pleiades, and the constellations of the southern sky.
¹⁰ He does great and unsearchable things,
wonders without number.

PSALM 147:3–5

³ He heals the brokenhearted
and bandages their wounds.
⁴ He counts the number of the stars;
he gives names to all of them.
⁵ Our Lord is great, vast in power;
his understanding is infinite.

ISAIAH 40:26–29

²⁶ Look up and see!
Who created these?
He brings out the stars by number;
he calls all of them by name.
Because of his great power and strength,
not one of them is missing.

²⁷ Jacob, why do you say,
and Israel, why do you assert,
"My way is hidden from the Lord,
and my claim is ignored by my God"?
²⁸ Do you not know?
Have you not heard?
The Lord is the everlasting God,
the Creator of the whole earth.
He never becomes faint or weary;
there is no limit to his understanding.
²⁹ He gives strength to the faint
and strengthens the powerless.

ROMANS 8:14–17

¹⁴ For all those led by God's Spirit are God's sons. ¹⁵ For you did not receive a spirit of slavery to fall back into fear. Instead, you received the Spirit of adoption, by whom we cry out, "*Abba*, Father!" ¹⁶ The Spirit himself testifies together with our spirit that we are God's children, ¹⁷ and if children, also heirs—heirs of God and coheirs with Christ—if indeed we suffer with him so that we may also be glorified with him.

HEBREWS 11:1–3, 8–16

LIVING BY FAITH

¹ Now faith is the reality of what is hoped for, the proof of what is not seen. ² For by this our ancestors were approved.

³ By faith we understand that the universe was created by the word of God, so that what is seen was made from things that are not visible.

…

⁸ By faith Abraham, when he was called, obeyed and set out for a place that he was going to receive as an inheritance. He went out, even though he did not know where he was going. ⁹ By faith he stayed as a foreigner in the land of promise, living in tents as did Isaac and Jacob, coheirs of the same promise. ¹⁰ For he was looking forward to the city that has foundations, whose architect and builder is God.

¹¹ By faith even Sarah herself, when she was unable to have children, received power to conceive offspring, even though she was past the age, since she considered that the one who had promised was faithful. ¹² Therefore, from one man—in fact, from one as good as dead—came offspring as numerous as the stars of the sky and as innumerable as the grains of sand along the seashore.

¹³ These all died in faith, although they had not received the things that were promised. But they saw them from a distance, greeted them, and confessed that they were foreigners and temporary residents on the earth. ¹⁴ Now those who say such things make it clear that they are seeking a homeland. ¹⁵ If they were thinking about where they came from, they would have had an opportunity to return. ¹⁶ But they now desire a better place—a heavenly one. Therefore, God is not ashamed to be called their God, for he has prepared a city for them.

In today's reading, what truths about God are reflected in creation?

Reflect on what creation demonstrates about God's nature, and write a prayer of praise in response.

Beaded Tassel Garland

TOTAL TIME
2 hours

DIFFICULTY
★ ☆ ☆

If you are looking for a festive craft to do alone or with a group of friends, this homemade tassel garland is an easy Scandinavian-inspired Christmas decoration!

WHAT YOU NEED

3½-inch cardboard piece

Scissors

Ruler or measuring tape

240 yards yarn in desired colors (We used Lily® Sugar'n Cream® yarn in ecru and sage green)

Tapestry needle

100 (20-millimeter) wooden beads

Hardware for hanging (optional)

WHAT TO DO

Place the cardboard piece in front of you. Cut a 4-inch piece of yarn and place it lengthwise along the top of your cardboard piece.

Wrap the remaining yarn 30 times around the cardboard from top to bottom, perpendicular to the 4-inch piece at the top. Then cut the yarn after the 30th wrap at the bottom of the bundle. Bring the ends of the 4-inch piece around the wrapped yarn and double knot the string. Leave the edges hanging over the top.

Slide the bundle off of the cardboard piece and cut through the end opposite the knot.

Cut another 4-inch piece of yarn and tie it around the bundle about 1 inch from the existing knot, trimming the ends.

Repeat until you have the desired number of tassels for your garland. (We made 32 tassels total, 16 of each color!)

Cut a length of yarn a little longer than your desired garland length (ours was 70 inches) and thread the tapestry needle. Determine the pattern you want to create with your colors sections. (Our pattern was to alternate between ecru and sage green, with 3 wooden beads between each tassel.)

Thread the wooden beads onto the yarn, tying a tassel on afterward using the excess string at the top of your tassel.

Knot the ends of your garland with a loop for hanging and trim all of the extra threads from tying your garland. Display on your mantle, on a wall, or around your Christmas tree!

DAY 10

The Bright and Morning Star

REVELATION 22:16

"I, Jesus, have sent my angel to attest these things to you for the churches. I am the Root and descendant of David, the bright morning star."

FULFILLED IN CHRIST
Luke 1:33

NUMBERS 24:17

I see him, but not now;
I perceive him, but not near.
A star will come from Jacob,
and a scepter will arise from Israel.
He will smash the forehead of Moab
and strike down all the Shethites.

FULFILLED IN CHRIST
Luke 1:32

2 SAMUEL 7:8–17

8 "So now this is what you are to say to my servant David: 'This is what the LORD of Armies says: I took you from the pasture, from tending the flock, to be ruler over my people Israel. 9 I have been with you wherever you have gone, and I have destroyed all your enemies before you. I will make a great name for you like that of the greatest on the earth. 10 I will designate a place for my people Israel and plant them, so that they may live there and not be disturbed again. Evildoers will not continue to oppress them as they have done 11 ever since the day I ordered judges to be over my people Israel. I will give you rest from all your enemies.

"'The LORD declares to you: The LORD himself will make a house for you. 12 When your time comes and you rest with your ancestors, I will raise up after you your descendant, who will come from your body, and I will establish his kingdom. 13 He is the one who will build a house for my name, and I will establish the throne of his kingdom forever. 14 I will be his father, and he will be my son. When he does wrong, I will discipline him with a rod of men and blows from mortals. 15 But my faithful love will never leave him as it did when I removed it from Saul, whom I removed from before you. 16 Your house and kingdom will endure before me forever, and your throne will be established forever.'"

17 Nathan reported all these words and this entire vision to David.

2 CHRONICLES 21:7

…but for the sake of the covenant the LORD had made with David, he was unwilling to destroy the house of David since the LORD had promised to give a lamp to David and to his sons forever.

MATTHEW 1:1–17

THE GENEALOGY OF JESUS CHRIST

1 An account of the genealogy of Jesus Christ, the Son of David, the Son of Abraham:

FROM ABRAHAM TO DAVID

2 Abraham fathered Isaac,
Isaac fathered Jacob,
Jacob fathered Judah and his brothers,
3 Judah fathered Perez and Zerah by Tamar,
Perez fathered Hezron,
Hezron fathered Aram,
4 Aram fathered Amminadab,
Amminadab fathered Nahshon,
Nahshon fathered Salmon,
5 Salmon fathered Boaz by Rahab,
Boaz fathered Obed by Ruth,
Obed fathered Jesse,
6 and Jesse fathered King David.

FROM DAVID TO THE BABYLONIAN EXILE

David fathered Solomon by Uriah's wife,
7 Solomon fathered Rehoboam,
Rehoboam fathered Abijah,
Abijah fathered Asa,
8 Asa fathered Jehoshaphat,
Jehoshaphat fathered Joram,
Joram fathered Uzziah,
9 Uzziah fathered Jotham,
Jotham fathered Ahaz,
Ahaz fathered Hezekiah,
10 Hezekiah fathered Manasseh,
Manasseh fathered Amon,
Amon fathered Josiah,
11 and Josiah fathered Jeconiah and his brothers
at the time of the exile to Babylon.

FROM THE EXILE TO THE MESSIAH

¹² After the exile to Babylon
Jeconiah fathered Shealtiel,
Shealtiel fathered Zerubbabel,
¹³ Zerubbabel fathered Abiud,
Abiud fathered Eliakim,
Eliakim fathered Azor,
¹⁴ Azor fathered Zadok,
Zadok fathered Achim,
Achim fathered Eliud,
¹⁵ Eliud fathered Eleazar,
Eleazar fathered Matthan,
Matthan fathered Jacob,
¹⁶ and Jacob fathered Joseph the husband of Mary, who gave birth to Jesus who is called the Messiah.

¹⁷ So all the generations from Abraham to David were fourteen generations; and from David until the exile to Babylon, fourteen generations; and from the exile to Babylon until the Messiah, fourteen generations.

2 PETER 1:19

We also have the prophetic word strongly confirmed, and you will do well to pay attention to it, as to a lamp shining in a dark place, until the day dawns and the morning star rises in your hearts.

How do the promises in today's reading point to Jesus?

Write a prayer asking God to make you more aware of how He fulfills every one of His promises.

DAY 10   DECEMBER 7, 2021

The Genealogy of Jesus

Jesus Christ was and is the long-anticipated Light of the World who came to earth, fully God and fully man.

The book of Matthew opens by showing Jesus's family history in the form of a genealogy. More than just a list of names, the genealogy shows God's faithfulness to work through ordinary, sinful people from generation to generation to bring Jesus, the bright morning star and eternal King, to redeem the nations. The following pages describe some unique features of this genealogy, while also highlighting the colorful history of key figures in Jesus's family tree along with biblical references for further reading.

The Genealogy of Jesus

① An account of the genealogy of Jesus Christ, the Son of David, the Son of Abraham:

— Time periods
— Explanation of term
— Key male ancestors
— Key female ancestors

FROM ABRAHAM TO DAVID

② Abraham fathered Isaac,

③ Isaac fathered Jacob,

④ Jacob fathered Judah and his brothers,

⑤ Judah fathered Perez and Zerah by Tamar, ⑥

Perez fathered Hezron,

Hezron fathered Aram,

Aram fathered Amminadab,

Amminadab fathered Nahshon,

⑦ Nahshon fathered Salmon,

Salmon fathered Boaz by Rahab, ⑧

⑨ Boaz fathered Obed by Ruth, ⑩

Obed fathered Jesse,

⑪ and Jesse fathered King David. ⑫

1. SON OF DAVID AND ABRAHAM

The book of Matthew was written to a Jewish audience who placed great value on lineage, connecting a person to their family of origin. The Old Testament promised that Abraham's descendants would bless the nations and that the Messiah would come from the line of David. Jesus, through the line of Joseph, was descended from both.

2. ABRAHAM

God established a covenant with Abraham and promised to make his descendants into a chosen nation, through whom the entire world would be blessed.
GN 11:27–31; 12:1–7; 15:1–21; 17:1–14

3. ISAAC

The first child of the promised nation. He was the initial fulfillment of God's promise to Abraham to give him a son and an heir.
GN 22:1–19; 25:11; 26:1–5, 12–25

4. JACOB

One of Isaac's twin sons, who wrestled with God and inherited the promises made to his father and grandfather. God changed his name to Israel, and his twelve sons began the twelve tribes of the nation Israel.
GN 27:1–40; 28:10–22; 32:3–32; 35:9–15

5. JUDAH

The fourth son of Jacob. Judah urged his brothers to sell his brother Joseph into slavery rather than kill him. Years later, after Joseph rose in power and tested his brothers, Judah offered his own life to protect his younger brother Benjamin. Later, Judah also slept with Tamar, his daughter-in-law, thinking she was a prostitute.
GN 37:26–28; 38; 44:14–34; 49:8–12

6. TAMAR

The Canaanite daughter-in-law of Judah, who deceived Judah after he failed to honor his commitment in order to bear a child belonging to the same family line as her deceased husband.
GN 38

7. NAHSHON

Nahshon was the leader of the tribe of Judah during Israel's desert wanderings.
NM 2:3; 7:12–17

8. RAHAB

A Canaanite prostitute in Jericho who hid the Israelite spies. Her loyalty to God was rewarded with a place among God's people.
JOS 2; 6:22–25

9. BOAZ

A relative of Ruth's mother-in-law, Naomi. After Ruth's husband died, Boaz married her and they had a son, enabling Ruth to carry on the family line of Naomi's husband.
RU 2; 3:1–15; 4:1–17

10. RUTH

A Moabite widow who remained loyal to her mother-in-law after her own husband's death by following her to Israel. There, God provided Ruth a husband and included Ruth's descendants in the line of kings through David.
RU 1–4

11. JESSE

The prophet Samuel sought out Jesse to anoint one of his sons as the future king of Israel after the first king, Saul, was rejected by God.
1SM 16:1, 6–13

12. KING

By referring to David as king, Matthew calls attention to the long line of kings Jesus descended from. Jesus was and is the true and better King of kings, a fulfillment of the royal Davidic line whose reign will last for eternity.

This genealogy includes the names of five women. It wasn't customary to include women in a Jewish genealogy, as the family line was carried through sons. Most scholars also believe that, other than Mary, the women included were not Jewish. The inclusion of women in this genealogy reinforces that the promised Messiah was a light to all nations and people, even those who were culturally marginalized.

FROM DAVID TO THE BABYLONIAN EXILE

⑬ David fathered Solomon by Uriah's wife, ⑭

⑮ Solomon fathered Rehoboam, ⑯

⑰ Rehoboam fathered Abijah,

Abijah fathered Asa,

Asa fathered Jehoshaphat,

Jehoshaphat fathered Joram,

Joram fathered Uzziah,

Uzziah fathered Jotham,

Jotham fathered Ahaz,

Ahaz fathered Hezekiah,

⑱ Hezekiah fathered Manasseh,

⑲ Manasseh fathered Amon,

Amon fathered Josiah,

⑳ and Josiah fathered Jeconiah and his brothers

㉑ at the time of the exile to Babylon.

— Time periods
— Explanation of term
— Key male ancestors
— Key female ancestors

13. DAVID

David succeeded Saul as the second king of Israel. During his life and reign, David disobeyed God on several occasions, including his sin against Bathsheba. But because of his posture of repentance before God, he was still called a man after God's heart.

1SM 13:14; 16–30; 2SM 1–24; 1KG 1–2;
1CH 2:13–15

14. URIAH'S WIFE

This refers to Bathsheba, a Hittite woman who was the wife of one of King David's most trusted warriors. After King David committed sexual sin against Bathsheba and she became pregnant, David had her husband Uriah killed in an attempt to cover up his sin. Later, Bathsheba became one of David's wives and gave birth to Solomon.

2SM 11:1–17, 26–27; 1KG 1:11–31

15. SOLOMON

The last king to reign over the united nation of Israel, who asked God for wisdom and led the construction of the first temple. He compromised his faithfulness to God in his later years by marrying hundreds of women who did not worship God and committing idolatry.

1KG 3; 8:54–66; 9:1–9; 11:1–13

16. A SERIES OF KINGS

Throughout the books of 1 & 2 Kings and 1 & 2 Chronicles, the kings in power were often described as either doing what was "evil" or "right in the LORD's sight" (2Ch 12:14; 20:32).

Rehoboam, Abijah, Joram, Uzziah, Jotham, Ahaz, Manasseh, Amon, and Jeconiah were all described as evil.

Asa, Jehoshaphat, Uzziah, Hezekiah, and Josiah were all described as faithful to God.

17. REHOBOAM

The first king of the southern kingdom of Judah after a civil war divided the united kingdom. Rehoboam enforced excessive labor on Israel, leading all the tribes except Judah and Benjamin to reject him as their king. He rejected God and led the people to worship other gods, including two golden calves.

1KG 12; 14:21–31; 2CH 10–12

18. HEZEKIAH

The twelfth king of Judah, who removed centers of idolatry Judah had used to worship other gods. God answered his prayer to deliver Jerusalem from the hands of another nation, Assyria.

2KG 18–19; 2CH 28:27–32:23, 30–33;
IS 36:1–37:37; 38:21–39:8

19. MANASSEH

Manasseh reinstituted the evil practices his father, Hezekiah, sought to remove from Judah, including corrupt religious practices and social injustices. Though Manasseh later repented, God still promised to bring about the exile of the people of Judah because of Manasseh's sin.

2KG 21:3–16; 23:26–27; 2CH 33:10–13

20. JOSIAH

The fifteenth king of Judah who sought religious reform and called the people of Judah to be faithful to their covenant with God.

2KG 21:24; 22:1–23:30; 2CH 33:25–35:25;
ZPH 1:1

21. AT THE TIME OF THE EXILE TO BABYLON

The exile marked a key point in Israel's history, reflecting God's discipline on the divided nations of Israel and Judah who had turned away from Him. Israel was taken into captivity in 722 BC by the nation of Assyria. Judah was later taken into captivity by Babylon in a series of defeats from 605 to 586 BC.

FROM THE EXILE TO THE MESSIAH

22 After the exile to Babylon

Jeconiah fathered Shealtiel,

Shealtiel fathered Zerubbabel,

23 Zerubbabel fathered Abiud,

Abiud fathered Eliakim,

Eliakim fathered Azor,

Azor fathered Zadok,

Zadok fathered Achim,

Achim fathered Eliud,

Eliud fathered Eleazar,

Eleazar fathered Matthan,

Matthan fathered Jacob,

24 and Jacob fathered Joseph the husband of Mary, 25

who gave birth to Jesus who is called the Messiah. 26

— Time periods
— Explanation of term
— Key male ancestors
— Key female ancestors

22. AFTER THE EXILE TO BABYLON

In 539 BC, the nation of Persia defeated Babylon, ending the legal exile of Judah. As part of Persia's victory, their king announced a decree allowing the exiles from Judah to return and rebuild the temple in Jerusalem that had been destroyed. While some exiles returned, not all did, leaving many dispersed throughout the land.

23. ZERUBBABEL

The governor of Judah after the Babylonian exile who helped to rebuild the temple in Jerusalem.

EZR 2:1-2; 4:2-3; 5:2; HG 1:1; 2:20-23

24. JOSEPH

Joseph was the husband of Mary, the mother of Jesus. After a visit from an angel, Joseph chose to remain betrothed to Mary even after she became pregnant. As Jesus's earthly father and Mary's husband, Joseph is Jesus's connection to the line of David.

See days 25 and 28

25. MARY

A young woman and the mother of Jesus. She is seen throughout Scripture at key events in Jesus's life, including His first miracle and His crucifixion. She also remained faithful to Jesus's mission after His death and resurrection.

See days 24 through 28
See also: JN 2:1-12; 19:17-30; AC 1:12-14

26. WHO IS CALLED THE MESSIAH

The title of "messiah" describes Jesus as the anointed, or chosen, one of Israel. In the same way that prophets, priests, and kings were ceremonially anointed to set them apart for their particular work, so too was Jesus set apart for His work of redemption. Unlike His lineage of imperfect human beings, Jesus lived a perfect and sinless life—the one, true Messiah.

The Consuming Fire 11

EXODUS 3:1–15

MOSES AND THE BURNING BUSH

¹ Meanwhile, Moses was shepherding the flock of his father-in-law Jethro, the priest of Midian. He led the flock to the far side of the wilderness and came to Horeb, the mountain of God. ² Then the angel of the Lord appeared to him in a flame of fire within a bush. As Moses looked, he saw that the bush was on fire but was not consumed. ³ So Moses thought, "I must go over and look at this remarkable sight. Why isn't the bush burning up?"

⁴ When the Lord saw that he had gone over to look, God called out to him from the bush, "Moses, Moses!"

"Here I am," he answered.

⁵ "Do not come closer," he said. "Remove the sandals from your feet, for the place where you are standing is holy ground." ⁶ Then he continued, "I am the God of your father, the God of Abraham, the God of Isaac, and the God of Jacob." Moses hid his face because he was afraid to look at God.

⁷ Then the Lord said, "I have observed the misery of my people in Egypt, and have heard them crying out because of their oppressors.

I know about their sufferings, ⁸ and I have come down to rescue them from the power of the Egyptians and to bring them from that land to a good and spacious land, a land flowing with milk and honey—

the territory of the Canaanites, Hethites, Amorites, Perizzites, Hivites, and Jebusites. ⁹ So because the Israelites' cry for help has come to me, and I have also seen the way the Egyptians are oppressing them, ¹⁰ therefore, go. I am sending you to Pharaoh so that you may lead my people, the Israelites, out of Egypt."

¹¹ But Moses asked God, "Who am I that I should go to Pharaoh and that I should bring the Israelites out of Egypt?"

¹² He answered, "I will certainly be with you, and this will be the sign to you that I am the one who sent you: when you bring the people out of Egypt, you will all worship God at this mountain."

¹³ Then Moses asked God, "If I go to the Israelites and say to them, 'The God of your ancestors has sent me to you,' and they ask me, 'What is his name?' what should I tell them?"

¹⁴ God replied to Moses, "I AM WHO I AM. This is what you are to say to the Israelites: I AM has sent me to you." ¹⁵ God also said to Moses, "Say this to the Israelites: The Lord, the God of your ancestors, the God of Abraham, the God of Isaac, and the God of Jacob, has sent me to you. This is my name forever; this is how I am to be remembered in every generation."

ISAIAH 30:27–30

²⁷ Look! The name of the Lord is coming from far away,
his anger burning and heavy with smoke.
His lips are full of fury,
and his tongue is like a consuming fire.
²⁸ His breath is like an overflowing torrent
that rises to the neck.
He comes to sift the nations in a sieve of destruction
and to put a bridle on the jaws of the peoples
to lead them astray.
²⁹ Your singing will be like that
on the night of a holy festival,
and your heart will rejoice
like one who walks to the music of a flute,
going up to the mountain of the Lord,
to the Rock of Israel.
³⁰ And the Lord will make the splendor of his voice heard
and reveal his arm striking in angry wrath
and a flame of consuming fire,
in driving rain, a torrent, and hailstones.

ACTS 2:1–4

¹ When the day of Pentecost had arrived, they were all together in one place. ² Suddenly a sound like that of a violent rushing wind came from heaven, and it filled the whole house where they were staying. ³ They saw tongues like

NOTES

flames of fire that separated and rested on each one of them. ⁴ Then they were all filled with the Holy Spirit and began to speak in different tongues, as the Spirit enabled them.

HEBREWS 12:18–29

¹⁸ For you have not come to what could be touched, to a blazing fire, to darkness, gloom, and storm, ¹⁹ to the blast of a trumpet, and the sound of words. Those who heard it begged that not another word be spoken to them, ²⁰ for they could not bear what was commanded: If even an animal touches the mountain, it must be stoned. ²¹ The appearance was so terrifying that Moses said, I am trembling with fear. ²² Instead, you have come to Mount Zion, to the city of the living God (the heavenly Jerusalem), to myriads of angels, a festive gathering, ²³ to the assembly of the firstborn whose names have been written in heaven, to a Judge, who is God of all, to the spirits of righteous people made perfect, ²⁴ and to Jesus, the mediator of a new covenant, and to the sprinkled blood, which says better things than the blood of Abel.

²⁵ See to it that you do not reject the one who speaks. For if they did not escape when they rejected him who warned them on earth, even less will we if we turn away from him who warns us from heaven. ²⁶ His voice shook the earth at that time, but now he has promised, Yet once more I will shake not only the earth but also the heavens. ²⁷ This expression, "Yet once more," indicates the removal of what can be shaken—that is, created things—so that what is not shaken might remain. ²⁸ Therefore, since we are receiving a kingdom that cannot be shaken, let us be thankful. By it, we may serve God acceptably, with reverence and awe, ²⁹ for our God is a consuming fire.

How is God described in today's reading?

Write a prayer of praise reflecting on what you learned about God's character today.

DAY 11

DECEMBER 8, 2021

DAY 12

Light in the Darkness

EXODUS 10:21–23

THE NINTH PLAGUE: DARKNESS

²¹ Then the LORD said to Moses, "Stretch out your hand toward heaven, and there will be darkness over the land of Egypt, a darkness that can be felt." ²² So Moses stretched out his hand toward heaven, and there was thick darkness throughout the land of Egypt for three days. ²³ One person could not see another, and for three days they did not move from where they were. Yet all the Israelites had light where they lived.

EXODUS 13:17–22

¹⁷ When Pharaoh let the people go, God did not lead them along the road to the land of the Philistines, even though it was nearby; for God said, "The people will change their minds and return to Egypt if they face war." ¹⁸ So he led the people around toward the Red Sea along the road of the wilderness. And the Israelites left the land of Egypt in battle formation.

¹⁹ Moses took the bones of Joseph with him, because Joseph had made the Israelites swear a solemn oath, saying, "God will certainly come to your aid; then you must take my bones with you from this place."

²⁰ They set out from Succoth and camped at Etham on the edge of the wilderness. ²¹ The LORD went ahead of them in a pillar of cloud to lead them on their way during the day and in a pillar of fire to give them light at night, so that they could travel day or night. ²² The pillar of cloud by day and the pillar of fire by night never left its place in front of the people.

PSALM 18:1–19, 25–32

PRAISE FOR DELIVERANCE

For the choir director. Of the servant of the LORD, David, who spoke the words of this song to the LORD on the day the LORD rescued him from the grasp of all his enemies and from the power of Saul. He said:

¹ I love you, LORD, my strength.
² The LORD is my rock,
my fortress, and my deliverer,
my God, my rock where I seek refuge,
my shield and the horn of my salvation,
my stronghold.
³ I called to the LORD, who is worthy of praise,
and I was saved from my enemies.

⁴ The ropes of death were wrapped around me;
the torrents of destruction terrified me.
⁵ The ropes of Sheol entangled me;
the snares of death confronted me.
⁶ I called to the LORD in my distress,
and I cried to my God for help.
From his temple he heard my voice,
and my cry to him reached his ears.

⁷ Then the earth shook and quaked;
the foundations of the mountains trembled;
they shook because he burned with anger.
⁸ Smoke rose from his nostrils,
and consuming fire came from his mouth;
coals were set ablaze by it.
⁹ He bent the heavens and came down,
total darkness beneath his feet.
¹⁰ He rode on a cherub and flew,
soaring on the wings of the wind.
¹¹ He made darkness his hiding place,
dark storm clouds his canopy around him.
¹² From the radiance of his presence,
his clouds swept onward with hail and blazing coals.
¹³ The LORD thundered from heaven;
the Most High made his voice heard.
¹⁴ He shot his arrows and scattered them;
he hurled lightning bolts and routed them.

¹⁵ The depths of the sea became visible,
the foundations of the world were exposed,
at your rebuke, Lord,
at the blast of the breath of your nostrils.

¹⁶ He reached down from on high
and took hold of me;
he pulled me out of deep water.
¹⁷ He rescued me from my powerful enemy
and from those who hated me,
for they were too strong for me.
¹⁸ They confronted me in the day of my calamity,
but the Lord was my support.
¹⁹ He brought me out to a spacious place;
he rescued me because he delighted in me.

…

²⁵ With the faithful
you prove yourself faithful,
with the blameless
you prove yourself blameless,
²⁶ with the pure
you prove yourself pure,
but with the crooked
you prove yourself shrewd.
²⁷ For you rescue an oppressed people,
but you humble those with haughty eyes.
²⁸ Lord, you light my lamp;
my God illuminates my darkness.

²⁹ With you I can attack a barricade,
and with my God I can leap over a wall.

³⁰ God—his way is perfect;
the word of the Lord is pure.
He is a shield to all who take refuge in him.
³¹ For who is God besides the Lord?
And who is a rock? Only our God.
³² God—he clothes me with strength
and makes my way perfect.

EPHESIANS 5:8–17

⁸ For you were once darkness, but now you are light in the Lord. Walk as children of light— ⁹ for the fruit of the light consists of all goodness, righteousness, and truth— ¹⁰ testing what is pleasing to the Lord. ¹¹ Don't participate in the fruitless works of darkness, but instead expose them. ¹² For it is shameful even to mention what is done by them in secret. ¹³ Everything exposed by the light is made visible, ¹⁴ for what makes everything visible is light. Therefore it is said:

> Get up, sleeper, and rise up from the dead,
> and Christ will shine on you.

¹⁵ Pay careful attention, then, to how you walk—not as unwise people but as wise— ¹⁶ making the most of the time, because the days are evil. ¹⁷ So don't be foolish, but understand what the Lord's will is.

How is light a guiding presence in today's reading?

Write a prayer of gratitude for how God has led you through a dark season.

The First Noel

WORDS
Traditional English carol

MUSIC
Traditional English carol; last chorus setting and choral ending by Dennis Allen

The Light of His Glory

13

EXODUS 33:12–23

THE LORD'S GLORY

[12] Moses said to the Lord, "Look, you have told me, 'Lead this people up,' but you have not let me know whom you will send with me. You said, 'I know you by name, and you have also found favor with me.' [13] Now if I have indeed found favor with you, please teach me your ways, and I will know you, so that I may find favor with you. Now consider that this nation is your people."

[14] And he replied,

"My presence will go with you, and I will give you rest."

[15] "If your presence does not go," Moses responded to him, "don't make us go up from here. [16] How will it be known that I and your people have found favor with you unless you go with us? I and your people will be distinguished by this from all the other people on the face of the earth."

[17] The Lord answered Moses, "I will do this very thing you have asked, for you have found favor with me, and I know you by name."

[18] Then Moses said, "Please, let me see your glory."

[19] He said, "I will cause all my goodness to pass in front of you, and I will proclaim the name 'the Lord' before you. I will be gracious to whom I will be gracious, and I will have compassion on whom I will have compassion." [20] But he added, "You cannot see my face, for humans cannot see me and live." [21] The Lord said, "Here is a place near me. You are to stand on the rock, [22] and when my glory passes by, I will put you in the crevice of the rock and cover you with my hand until I have passed by. [23] Then I will take my hand away, and you will see my back, but my face will not be seen."

EXODUS 34:5–9, 29–35

⁵ The Lord came down in a cloud, stood with him there, and proclaimed his name, "the Lord." ⁶ The Lord passed in front of him and proclaimed:

> The Lord—the Lord is a compassionate and gracious God, slow to anger and abounding in faithful love and truth, ⁷ maintaining faithful love to a thousand generations, forgiving iniquity, rebellion, and sin. But he will not leave the guilty unpunished, bringing the consequences of the fathers' iniquity on the children and grandchildren to the third and fourth generation.

⁸ Moses immediately knelt low on the ground and worshiped. ⁹ Then he said, "My Lord, if I have indeed found favor with you, my Lord, please go with us (even though this is a stiff-necked people), forgive our iniquity and our sin, and accept us as your own possession."

…

MOSES'S RADIANT FACE

²⁹ As Moses descended from Mount Sinai—with the two tablets of the testimony in his hands as he descended the mountain—he did not realize that the skin of his face shone as a result of his speaking with the Lord. ³⁰ When Aaron and all the Israelites saw Moses, the skin of his face shone! They were afraid to come near him. ³¹ But Moses called out to them, so Aaron and all the leaders of the community returned to him, and Moses spoke to them. ³² Afterward all the Israelites came near, and he commanded them to do everything the Lord had told him on Mount Sinai. ³³ When Moses had finished speaking with them, he put a veil over his face. ³⁴ But whenever Moses went before the Lord to speak with him, he would remove the veil until he came out. After he came out, he would tell the Israelites what he had been commanded, ³⁵ and the Israelites would see that Moses's face was radiant. Then Moses would put the veil over his face again until he went to speak with the Lord.

DANIEL 12:3

Those who have insight will shine
like the bright expanse of the heavens,
and those who lead many to righteousness,
like the stars forever and ever.

MATTHEW 17:1–7

THE TRANSFIGURATION

¹ After six days Jesus took Peter, James, and his brother John and led them up on a high mountain by themselves. ² He was transfigured in front of them, and his face shone like the sun; his clothes became as white as the light. ³ Suddenly, Moses

and Elijah appeared to them, talking with him. ⁴ Then Peter said to Jesus, "Lord, it's good for us to be here. If you want, I will set up three shelters here: one for you, one for Moses, and one for Elijah."

⁵ While he was still speaking, suddenly a bright cloud covered them, and a voice from the cloud said, "This is my beloved Son, with whom I am well-pleased. Listen to him!" ⁶ When the disciples heard this, they fell facedown and were terrified.

⁷ Jesus came up, touched them, and said, "Get up; don't be afraid."

2 CORINTHIANS 3:7–18

NEW COVENANT MINISTRY

⁷ Now if the ministry that brought death, chiseled in letters on stones, came with glory, so that the Israelites were not able to gaze steadily at Moses's face because of its glory, which was set aside, ⁸ how will the ministry of the Spirit not be more glorious? ⁹ For if the ministry that brought condemnation had glory, the ministry that brings righteousness overflows with even more glory. ¹⁰ In fact, what had been glorious is not glorious now by comparison because of the glory that surpasses it. ¹¹ For if what was set aside was glorious, what endures will be even more glorious.

¹² Since, then, we have such a hope, we act with great boldness. ¹³ We are not like Moses, who used to put a veil over his face to prevent the Israelites from gazing steadily until the end of the glory of what was being set aside, ¹⁴ but their minds were hardened. For to this day, at the reading of the old covenant, the same veil remains; it is not lifted, because it is set aside only in Christ. ¹⁵ Yet still today, whenever Moses is read, a veil lies over their hearts, ¹⁶ but whenever a person turns to the Lord, the veil is removed. ¹⁷ Now the Lord is the Spirit, and where the Spirit of the Lord is, there is freedom. ¹⁸ We all, with unveiled faces, are looking as in a mirror at the glory of the Lord and are being transformed into the same image from glory to glory; this is from the Lord who is the Spirit.

How is God's glory displayed as light in today's reading?

Write a prayer asking God to make you a reflection of His glory to those around you this Advent and beyond.

DAY 13   DECEMBER 10, 2021

Roasted Butternut Squash Soup

PREP TIME
20 minutes

COOK TIME
1 hour and 15 minutes

YIELDS
4 servings

DIFFICULTY
★ ★ ☆

A note from Chef Simoni:

The caramelization of the squash gives this soup a unique depth and texture. This integrates the sweetness of squash with the acidity of sherry vinegar to create a velvety and delightful soup.

INGREDIENTS

SQUASH

1 (4 to 5 pound) butternut squash

Canola oil, to coat squash

1 ½ teaspoons salt

1 teaspoon pepper

SOUP BASE

2 tablespoons canola oil

3 cloves garlic

1 large white onion, diced large

1 package of thyme, tied tightly together with butcher or kitchen twine

4 ½ cups water

1 ½ teaspoons cumin

½ teaspoon cardamom

¼ cup honey

¼ cup sherry vinegar

3 bay leaves

ADDITIONAL SEASONINGS

Salt, to taste

Pepper, to taste

Honey, to taste

Chives, garnish

METHOD

Preheat the oven to 375°F.

Using a peeler, remove the exterior of the squash. (We recommend wearing gloves during this step.) Cut the squash in half, lengthwise, and remove the seeds. Then cut the squash into 4 even segments per half.

Line a baking sheet with foil and coat the squash in canola oil. Apply salt and pepper, then roast for 25 minutes. The squash should be tender and slightly browned from the roasting process.

Heat canola oil in a 4-quart dutch oven over medium heat. Cook the garlic, onion, and thyme for 5 minutes. Add the rest of the ingredients including the squash, then reduce the heat to low and simmer for 45 minutes.

Remove the bundle of thyme and bay leaves. Working in small batches because of the hot liquid, puree the mixture in a blender and set aside in a large soup bowl.

Season the mixture with some salt, pepper, and honey to taste. Garnish with chives. Serve hot.

Chef Simoni has cooked this twice for the She Reads Truth Christmas party. Both times, this soup was the talk of the night!

Grace Day

DAY 14

DECEMBER 11, 2021

Advent is a season of celebration and contemplation. We rejoice that our Savior has come to us! We also seek unhurried moments of quiet to reflect on His wondrous light and the promise of His future return. Take time today to pause from the busyness of the season to catch up on your reading, make space for prayer, and rest in God's presence.

I see him, but not now;
I perceive him, but not near.
A star will come from Jacob,
and a scepter will arise from Israel.

NUMBERS 24:17

DAY 15

A PRAYER FOR

the Third Sunday of Advent

Arise, shine, for your light has come,
and the glory of the Lord shines over you.
For look, darkness will cover the earth,
and total darkness the peoples;
but the Lord will shine over you,
and his glory will appear over you.
Nations will come to your light,
and kings to your shining brightness.

ISAIAH 60:1–3

DECEMBER 12, 2021

Lord Jesus,
Master of both the light and the darkness, send Your Holy
Spirit upon our preparations for Christmas.
We who have so much to do and seek quiet spaces to hear
Your voice each day,
We who are anxious over many things look forward to Your
coming among us.
We who are blessed in so many ways long for the complete joy
of Your kingdom.
We whose hearts are heavy seek the joy of Your presence.
We are Your people, walking in darkness, yet seeking the light.
To You we say, "Come Lord Jesus!"
Amen.

HENRI J.M. NOUWEN

ADVENT CANDLES

What is the history of Advent candles?

Advent candles originated in the early 1800s when Johann Hinrich Wichern, a minister in Germany, created the first Advent wreath from an old cart wheel to give the children in his ministry a way to count down the days until Christmas. Wichern placed twenty-four Advent candles in this wreath: twenty red candles that were lit throughout the week, and four white candles to light each Sunday during Advent.

Many Christians now mark the four Sundays during Advent by lighting one candle each Sunday, and a fifth candle on Christmas Eve. The colors of these candles vary between denominations, but many Protestant traditions use three purple or blue candles (the traditional Church color for Advent), one pink candle, and one white candle. The purple candles represent the themes of hope, faith, and peace. The pink candle represents the theme of joy, and the white candle represents the light and life of Christ.

The Source of Light and Life

16

JOHN 12:46–50

⁴⁶ "I have come as light into the world, so that everyone who believes in me would not remain in darkness. ⁴⁷ If anyone hears my words and doesn't keep them, I do not judge him; for I did not come to judge the world but to save the world. ⁴⁸ The one who rejects me and doesn't receive my sayings has this as his judge: The word I have spoken will judge him on the last day. ⁴⁹ For I have not spoken on my own, but the Father himself who sent me has given me a command to say everything I have said. ⁵⁰ I know that his command is eternal life. So the things that I speak, I speak just as the Father has told me."

JOHN 14:6

Jesus told him, "I am the way, the truth, and the life. No one comes to the Father except through me."

ISAIAH 60:1–3

¹ Arise, shine, for your light has come,
and the glory of the Lord shines over you.
² For look, darkness will cover the earth,
and total darkness the peoples;
but the Lord will shine over you,
and his glory will appear over you.
³ Nations will come to your light,
and kings to your shining brightness.

2 CORINTHIANS 4:1–6

THE LIGHT OF THE GOSPEL

¹ Therefore, since we have this ministry because we were shown mercy, we do not give up. ² Instead, we have renounced secret and shameful things, not acting deceitfully or distorting the word of God, but commending ourselves before God

to everyone's conscience by an open display of the truth. ³ But if our gospel is veiled, it is veiled to those who are perishing. ⁴ In their case, the god of this age has blinded the minds of the unbelievers to keep them from seeing the light of the gospel of the glory of Christ, who is the image of God. ⁵ For we are not proclaiming ourselves but Jesus Christ as Lord, and ourselves as your servants for Jesus's sake. ⁶ For God who said, "Let light shine out of darkness," has shone in our hearts to give the light of the knowledge of God's glory in the face of Jesus Christ.

REVELATION 1:12–20

¹² Then I turned to see whose voice it was that spoke to me. When I turned I saw seven golden lampstands, ¹³ and among the lampstands was one like the Son of Man, dressed in a robe and with a golden sash wrapped around his chest. ¹⁴ The hair of his head was white as wool—white as snow—and his eyes like a fiery flame. ¹⁵ His feet were like fine bronze as it is fired in a furnace, and his voice like the sound of cascading waters. ¹⁶ He had seven stars in his right hand; a sharp double-edged sword came from his mouth, and his face was shining like the sun at full strength.

¹⁷ When I saw him, I fell at his feet like a dead man. He laid his right hand on me and said, "Don't be afraid. I am the First and the Last, ¹⁸ and the Living One. I was dead, but look—I am alive forever and ever, and I hold the keys of death and Hades. ¹⁹ Therefore write what you have seen, what is, and what will take place after this. ²⁰ The mystery of the seven stars you saw in my right hand and of the seven golden lampstands is this: The seven stars are the angels of the seven churches, and the seven lampstands are the seven churches."

According to today's reading, how is Jesus the source of light and life?

Write a prayer praising Jesus as the only true source of light and life, who has come to us and has promised to come again.

DAY 16   DECEMBER 13, 2021

SECTION

2

PEOPLE OF THE LIGHT

You are all children of light and children of the day.

1 THESSALONIANS 5:5

We do not sit on the sidelines of the story of redemption. We celebrate the first advent and eagerly anticipate the second because the incarnation changes everything—including us. Those who are in Jesus share in His call to be light to the world, a reflection of Him through the work of His Spirit. As we move toward Christmas Day, we'll read Scripture calling us to respond to the arrival of our Savior by living as shining lights in this dark world.

Seeing the Light   17

JOHN 9:1–7, 13–41

THE SIXTH SIGN: HEALING A MAN BORN BLIND

¹ As he was passing by, he saw a man blind from birth. ² His disciples asked him, "Rabbi, who sinned, this man or his parents, that he was born blind?"

³ "Neither this man nor his parents sinned," Jesus answered. "This came about so that God's works might be displayed in him. ⁴ We must do the works of him who sent me while it is day. Night is coming when no one can work. ⁵ As long as I am in the world, I am the light of the world."

⁶ After he said these things he spit on the ground, made some mud from the saliva, and spread the mud on his eyes. ⁷ "Go," he told him, "wash in the pool of Siloam" (which means "Sent"). So he left, washed, and came back seeing.

…

THE HEALED MAN'S TESTIMONY

¹³ They brought the man who used to be blind to the Pharisees. ¹⁴ The day that Jesus made the mud and opened his eyes was a Sabbath. ¹⁵ Then the Pharisees asked him again how he received his sight.

"He put mud on my eyes," he told them. "I washed and I can see."

¹⁶ Some of the Pharisees said, "This man is not from God, because he doesn't keep the Sabbath." But others were saying, "How can a sinful man perform such signs?" And there was a division among them.

¹⁷ Again they asked the blind man, "What do you say about him, since he opened your eyes?"

"He's a prophet," he said.

¹⁸ The Jews did not believe this about him—that he was blind and received sight—until they summoned the parents of the one who had received his sight.

¹⁹ They asked them, "Is this your son, the one you say was born blind? How then does he now see?"

²⁰ "We know this is our son and that he was born blind," his parents answered. ²¹ "But we don't know how he now sees, and we don't know who opened his eyes. Ask him; he's of age. He will speak for himself." ²² His parents said these things because they were afraid of the Jews, since the Jews had already agreed that if anyone confessed him as the Messiah, he would be banned from the synagogue. ²³ This is why his parents said, "He's of age; ask him."

²⁴ So a second time they summoned the man who had been blind and told him, "Give glory to God. We know that this man is a sinner."

²⁵ He answered, "Whether or not he's a sinner, I don't know.

One thing I do know: I was blind, and now I can see!"

²⁶ Then they asked him, "What did he do to you? How did he open your eyes?"

²⁷ "I already told you," he said, "and you didn't listen. Why do you want to hear it again? You don't want to become his disciples too, do you?"

²⁸ They ridiculed him: "You're that man's disciple, but we're Moses's disciples. ²⁹ We know that God has spoken to Moses. But this man—we don't know where he's from."

³⁰ "This is an amazing thing!" the man told them. "You don't know where he is from, and yet he opened my eyes. ³¹ We know that God doesn't listen to sinners, but if anyone is God-fearing and does his will, he listens to him. ³² Throughout history no one has ever heard of someone opening the eyes of a person born blind. ³³ If this man were not from God, he wouldn't be able to do anything."

³⁴ "You were born entirely in sin," they replied, "and are you trying to teach us?" Then they threw him out.

SPIRITUAL BLINDNESS

³⁵ Jesus heard that they had thrown the man out, and when he found him, he asked, "Do you believe in the Son of Man?"

³⁶ "Who is he, Sir, that I may believe in him?" he asked.

³⁷ Jesus answered, "You have seen him; in fact, he is the one speaking with you."

³⁸ "I believe, Lord!" he said, and he worshiped him.

³⁹ Jesus said, "I came into this world for judgment, in order that those who do not see will see and those who do see will become blind."

⁴⁰ Some of the Pharisees who were with him heard these things and asked him, "We aren't blind too, are we?"

⁴¹ "If you were blind," Jesus told them, "you wouldn't have sin. But now that you say, 'We see,' your sin remains."

ACTS 9:1–20

THE DAMASCUS ROAD

¹ Now Saul was still breathing threats and murder against the disciples of the Lord. He went to the high priest ² and requested letters from him to the synagogues in Damascus, so that if he found any men or women who belonged to the Way, he might bring them as prisoners to Jerusalem. ³ As he traveled and was nearing Damascus, a light from heaven suddenly flashed around him. ⁴ Falling to the ground, he heard a voice saying to him, "Saul, Saul, why are you persecuting me?"

⁵ "Who are you, Lord?" Saul said.

"I am Jesus, the one you are persecuting," he replied. ⁶ "But get up and go into the city, and you will be told what you must do."

⁷ The men who were traveling with him stood speechless, hearing the sound but seeing no one. ⁸ Saul got up from the ground, and though his eyes were open, he could see nothing. So they took him by the hand and led him into Damascus. ⁹ He was unable to see for three days and did not eat or drink.

SAUL'S BAPTISM

¹⁰ There was a disciple in Damascus named Ananias, and the Lord said to him in a vision, "Ananias."

"Here I am, Lord," he replied.

¹¹ "Get up and go to the street called Straight," the Lord said to him, "to the house of Judas, and ask for a man from Tarsus named Saul, since he is praying there. ¹² In a vision he has seen a man named Ananias coming in and placing his hands on him so that he may regain his sight."

¹³ "Lord," Ananias answered, "I have heard from many people about this man, how much harm he has done to your saints in Jerusalem. ¹⁴ And he has authority here from the chief priests to arrest all who call on your name."

¹⁵ But the Lord said to him, "Go, for this man is my chosen instrument to take my name to Gentiles, kings, and Israelites. ¹⁶ I will show him how much he must suffer for my name."

¹⁷ Ananias went and entered the house. He placed his hands on him and said, "Brother Saul, the Lord Jesus, who appeared to you on the road you were traveling, has sent me so that you may regain your sight and be filled with the Holy Spirit."

¹⁸ At once something like scales fell from his eyes, and he regained his sight. Then he got up and was baptized. ¹⁹ And after taking some food, he regained his strength.

SAUL PROCLAIMING THE MESSIAH

Saul was with the disciples in Damascus for some time. ²⁰ Immediately he began proclaiming Jesus in the synagogues: "He is the Son of God."

ACTS 26:12–18

PAUL'S ACCOUNT OF HIS CONVERSION AND COMMISSION

¹² I was traveling to Damascus under these circumstances with authority and a commission from the chief priests. ¹³ King Agrippa, while on the road at midday, I saw a light from heaven brighter than the sun, shining around me and those traveling with me. ¹⁴ We all fell to the ground, and I heard a voice speaking to me in Aramaic, "Saul, Saul, why are you persecuting me? It is hard for you to kick against the goads."

¹⁵ I asked, "Who are you, Lord?"

And the Lord replied, "I am Jesus, the one you are persecuting. ¹⁶ But get up and stand on your feet. For I have appeared to you for this purpose, to appoint you as a servant and a witness of what you have seen and will see of me. ¹⁷ I will rescue you from your people and from the Gentiles. I am sending you to them ¹⁸ to open their eyes so that they may turn from darkness to light and from the power of Satan to God, that they may receive forgiveness of sins and a share among those who are sanctified by faith in me."

COLOSSIANS 1:9–14

PRAYER FOR SPIRITUAL GROWTH

⁹ For this reason also, since the day we heard this, we haven't stopped praying for you. We are asking that you may be filled with the knowledge of his will in all wisdom and spiritual understanding, ¹⁰ so that you may walk worthy of the Lord, fully pleasing to him: bearing fruit in every good work and growing in the knowledge of God, ¹¹ being strengthened with all power, according to his glorious might, so that you may have great endurance and patience, joyfully ¹² giving thanks to the Father, who has enabled you to share in the saints' inheritance in the light. ¹³ He has rescued us from the domain of darkness and transferred us into the kingdom of the Son he loves. ¹⁴ In him we have redemption, the forgiveness of sins.

What was the cause of each example of blindness in today's reading? Reflect on your own life, listing areas where Jesus has opened your eyes.

___

___

___

___

___

___

___

___

___

___

___

___

DAY 17   DECEMBER 14, 2021

O Come, All Ye Faithful

WORDS
Original Latin by John Francis Wade; translation by Frederick Oakeley

MUSIC
John Francis Wade; harmony from *The English Hymnal*

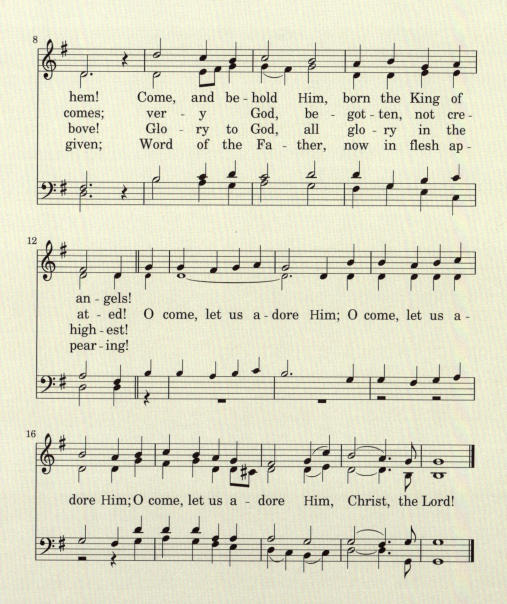

DAY 18

Walking in the Light

JOHN 12:23–36

²³ Jesus replied to them, "The hour has come for the Son of Man to be glorified. ²⁴ Truly I tell you, unless a grain of wheat falls to the ground and dies, it remains by itself. But if it dies, it produces much fruit. ²⁵ The one who loves his life will lose it, and the one who hates his life in this world will keep it for eternal life. ²⁶ If anyone serves me, he must follow me. Where I am, there my servant also will be. If anyone serves me, the Father will honor him.

²⁷ "Now my soul is troubled. What should I say—Father, save me from this hour? But that is why I came to this hour. ²⁸ Father, glorify your name."

Then a voice came from heaven: "I have glorified it, and I will glorify it again."

²⁹ The crowd standing there heard it and said it was thunder. Others said, "An angel has spoken to him."

³⁰ Jesus responded, "This voice came, not for me, but for you. ³¹ Now is the judgment of this world. Now the ruler of this world will be cast out. ³² As for me, if I am lifted up from the earth I will draw all people to myself." ³³ He said this to indicate what kind of death he was about to die.

³⁴ Then the crowd replied to him, "We have heard from the law that the Messiah will remain forever. So how can you say, 'The Son of Man must be lifted up'? Who is this Son of Man?"

³⁵ Jesus answered, "The light will be with you only a little longer. Walk while you have the light so that darkness doesn't overtake you. The one who walks in darkness doesn't know where he's going. ³⁶ While you have the light,

believe in the light so that you may become children of light."

Jesus said this, then went away and hid from them.

PROVERBS 4:18

The path of the righteous is like the light of dawn, shining brighter and brighter until midday.

1 THESSALONIANS 5:5

For you are all children of light and children of the day. We do not belong to the night or the darkness.

1 PETER 2:9–10

⁹ But you are a chosen race, a royal priesthood, a holy nation, a people for his possession, so that you may proclaim the praises of the one who called you out of darkness into his marvelous light. ¹⁰ Once you were not a people, but now you are God's people; you had not received mercy, but now you have received mercy.

1 JOHN 1:5–10

FELLOWSHIP WITH GOD

⁵ This is the message we have heard from him and declare to you: God is light, and there is absolutely no darkness in

him. ⁶ If we say, "We have fellowship with him," and yet we walk in darkness, we are lying and are not practicing the truth. ⁷ If we walk in the light as he himself is in the light, we have fellowship with one another, and the blood of Jesus his Son cleanses us from all sin. ⁸ If we say, "We have no sin," we are deceiving ourselves, and the truth is not in us. ⁹ If we confess our sins, he is faithful and righteous to forgive us our sins and to cleanse us from all unrighteousness. ¹⁰ If we say, "We have not sinned," we make him a liar, and his word is not in us.

1 JOHN 2:8–11

⁸ Yet I am writing you a new command, which is true in him and in you, because the darkness is passing away and the true light is already shining.

⁹ The one who says he is in the light but hates his brother or sister is in the darkness until now.

¹⁰ The one who loves his brother or sister remains in the light, and there is no cause for stumbling in him. ¹¹ But the one who hates his brother or sister is in the darkness, walks in the darkness, and doesn't know where he's going, because the darkness has blinded his eyes.

What were Jesus's instructions in John 12? Reflect on how you can carry out these instructions as a bearer of gospel light in your life and community.

Reflecting the Light

MATTHEW 5:1–16

¹ When he saw the crowds, he went up on the mountain, and after he sat down, his disciples came to him. ² Then he began to teach them, saying:

THE BEATITUDES

³ "Blessed are the poor in spirit,
for the kingdom of heaven is theirs.
⁴ Blessed are those who mourn,
for they will be comforted.
⁵ Blessed are the humble,
for they will inherit the earth.
⁶ Blessed are those who hunger and thirst for righteousness,
for they will be filled.
⁷ Blessed are the merciful,
for they will be shown mercy.
⁸ Blessed are the pure in heart,
for they will see God.
⁹ Blessed are the peacemakers,
for they will be called sons of God.
¹⁰ Blessed are those who are persecuted because
of righteousness,
for the kingdom of heaven is theirs.

¹¹ "You are blessed when they insult you and persecute you and falsely say every kind of evil against you because of me. ¹² Be glad and rejoice, because your reward is great in heaven. For that is how they persecuted the prophets who were before you.

BELIEVERS ARE SALT AND LIGHT

¹³ "You are the salt of the earth. But if the salt should lose its taste, how can it be made salty? It's no longer good for anything but to be thrown out and trampled under people's feet.

¹⁴ "You are the light of the world. A city situated on a hill cannot be hidden. ¹⁵ No one lights a lamp and puts it under a basket, but rather on a lampstand, and it gives light for all who are in the house. ¹⁶ In the same way, let your light shine before others, so that they may see your good works and give glory to your Father in heaven."

ISAIAH 49:6–7

⁶ "It is not enough for you to be my servant
raising up the tribes of Jacob
and restoring the protected ones of Israel.

**I will also make you a light for
the nations,
to be my salvation to the ends of
the earth."**

⁷ This is what the LORD,
the Redeemer of Israel, his Holy One, says
to one who is despised,
to one abhorred by people,
to a servant of rulers:
"Kings will see, princes will stand up,
and they will all bow down
because of the LORD, who is faithful,
the Holy One of Israel—and he has chosen you."

EPHESIANS 4:17–24

LIVING THE NEW LIFE

¹⁷ Therefore, I say this and testify in the Lord: You should no longer walk as the Gentiles do, in the futility of their

thoughts. ⁱ⁸ They are darkened in their understanding, excluded from the life of God, because of the ignorance that is in them and because of the hardness of their hearts. ¹⁹ They became callous and gave themselves over to promiscuity for the practice of every kind of impurity with a desire for more and more.

²⁰ But that is not how you came to know Christ, ²¹ assuming you heard about him and were taught by him, as the truth is in Jesus, ²² to take off your former way of life, the old self that is corrupted by deceitful desires, ²³ to be renewed in the spirit of your minds, ²⁴ and to put on the new self, the one created according to God's likeness in righteousness and purity of the truth.

PHILIPPIANS 2:12–18

LIGHTS IN THE WORLD

¹² Therefore, my dear friends, just as you have always obeyed, so now, not only in my presence but even more in my absence, work out your own salvation with fear and trembling. ¹³ For it is God who is working in you both to will and to work according to his good purpose. ¹⁴ Do everything without grumbling and arguing, ¹⁵ so that you may be blameless and pure, children of God who are faultless in a crooked and perverted generation, among whom you shine like stars in the world, ¹⁶ by holding firm to the word of life. Then I can boast in the day of Christ that I didn't run or labor for nothing. ¹⁷ But even if I am poured out as a drink offering on the sacrificial service of your faith, I am glad and rejoice with all of you. ¹⁸ In the same way you should also be glad and rejoice with me.

What instructions are given to believers in today's reading? List ways you can respond to this call during the Advent season, and make a plan to put those opportunities into action.

DAY 19   DECEMBER 16, 2021

Prophecies of Jesus's Birth

From Genesis to Malachi, the Old Testament contains numerous prophecies about the birth of the Messiah. Here is a look at these Old Testament prophecies along with their New Testament fulfillment in Christ.

OLD TESTAMENT PROPHECY

FULFILLED IN CHRIST

"I will put hostility between you and the woman, and between your offspring and her offspring. He will strike your head, and you will strike his heel."

GN 3:15

"And all the nations of the earth will be blessed by your offspring because you have obeyed my command."

GN 22:18

Therefore, the Lord himself will give you a sign: See, the virgin will conceive, have a son, and name him Immanuel.

IS 7:14

When the time came to completion, God sent his Son, born of a woman, born under the law…

GL 4:4

An account of the genealogy of Jesus Christ, the Son of David, the Son of Abraham: Abraham fathered Isaac…

MT 1:1–2

In the sixth month, the angel Gabriel was sent by God to a town in Galilee called Nazareth, to a virgin engaged to a man named Joseph, of the house of David. The virgin's name was Mary.

LK 1:26–27

Now all this took place to fulfill what was spoken by the Lord through the prophet: See, the virgin will become pregnant and give birth to a son, and they will name him Immanuel, which is translated "God is with us."

MT 1:22–23

OLD TESTAMENT PROPHECY

I see him, but not now; I perceive him, but not near. A star will come from Jacob, and a scepter will arise from Israel.

NM 24:17

"When your time comes and you rest with your ancestors, I will raise up after you your descendant, who will come from your body, and I will establish his kingdom. He is the one who will build a house for my name, and I will establish the throne of his kingdom forever."

2SM 7:12–13

"In his days Judah will be saved, and Israel will dwell securely. This is the name he will be called: The Lord Is Our Righteousness."

JR 23:6

He will reign over the house of Jacob forever, and his kingdom will have no end.

LK 1:33

He will be great and will be called the Son of the Most High, and the Lord God will give him the throne of his father David.

LK 1:32

Today in the city of David a Savior was born for you, who is the Messiah, the Lord.

LK 2:11

FULFILLED IN CHRIST

Bethlehem Ephrathah, you are small among the clans of Judah; one will come from you to be ruler over Israel for me. His origin is from antiquity, from ancient times.

MC 5:2

"When Israel was a child, I loved him, and out of Egypt I called my son."

HS 11:1

This is what the Lord says: A voice was heard in Ramah, a lament with bitter weeping—Rachel weeping for her children, refusing to be comforted for her children because they are no more.

JR 31:15

When King Herod heard this, he was deeply disturbed, and all Jerusalem with him. So he assembled all the chief priests and scribes of the people and asked them where the Messiah would be born. "In Bethlehem of Judea," they told him, "because this is what was written by the prophet."

MT 2:3-5

So he got up, took the child and his mother during the night, and escaped to Egypt. He stayed there until Herod's death, so that what was spoken by the Lord through the prophet might be fulfilled: Out of Egypt I called my Son.

MT 2:14-15

Then Herod, when he realized that he had been outwitted by the wise men, flew into a rage. He gave orders to massacre all the boys in and around Bethlehem who were two years old and under, in keeping with the time he had learned from the wise men. Then what was spoken through Jeremiah the prophet was fulfilled.

MT 2:16-17

SECTION

3

THE LIGHT DAWNS

The people walking in darkness have seen a great light; a light has dawned on those living in the land of darkness.

ISAIAH 9:2

As we draw closer to Christmas Day, prepare your heart to read this familiar story through fresh eyes. Notice how light is present, from the star above the city of Bethlehem to the glory of God represented by the angels. Discover anew the dawning of the promised Light of the World in a baby boy born to a virgin, placed in a manger because there was no room in the inn.

CHRISTMAS CAROLING

Where does modern Christmas caroling come from?

While the angelic scene in Luke 2 is often recognized as the first celebration of Christmas through singing, our modern tradition of Christmas caroling can be traced back to the eighteenth and nineteenth centuries. Carolers would travel from home to home on Christmas Eve, pronouncing good cheer upon each home and singing carols about the nativity and other themes and activities associated with the Christmas season.

Light Overcomes the Darkness

ISAIAH 9:1–7

BIRTH OF THE PRINCE OF PEACE

¹ Nevertheless, the gloom of the distressed land will not be like that of the former times when he humbled the land of Zebulun and the land of Naphtali. But in the future he will bring honor to the way of the sea, to the land east of the Jordan, and to Galilee of the nations.

² The people walking in darkness
have seen a great light;
a light has dawned
on those living in the land of darkness.
³ You have enlarged the nation
and increased its joy.
The people have rejoiced before you
as they rejoice at harvest time
and as they rejoice when dividing spoils.
⁴ For you have shattered their oppressive yoke
and the rod on their shoulders,
the staff of their oppressor,
just as you did on the day of Midian.
⁵ For every trampling boot of battle
and the bloodied garments of war
will be burned as fuel for the fire.
⁶ For a child will be born for us,
a son will be given to us,
and the government will be on his shoulders.
He will be named
Wonderful Counselor, Mighty God,
Eternal Father, Prince of Peace.
⁷ The dominion will be vast,
and its prosperity will never end.
He will reign on the throne of David
and over his kingdom,
to establish and sustain it
with justice and righteousness from now on and forever.
The zeal of the LORD of Armies will accomplish this.

PSALM 27:1–6

¹ The LORD is my light and my salvation—
whom should I fear?
The LORD is the stronghold of my life—
whom should I dread?
² When evildoers came against me to devour my flesh,
my foes and my enemies stumbled and fell.
³ Though an army deploys against me,
my heart will not be afraid;
though a war breaks out against me,
I will still be confident.

⁴ I have asked one thing from the LORD;
it is what I desire:
to dwell in the house of the LORD
all the days of my life,
gazing on the beauty of the LORD
and seeking him in his temple.
⁵ For he will conceal me in his shelter
in the day of adversity;
he will hide me under the cover of his tent;
he will set me high on a rock.

⁶ Then my head will be high
above my enemies around me;
I will offer sacrifices in his tent with shouts of joy.
I will sing and make music to the Lord.

MICAH 7:8

Do not rejoice over me, my enemy!
Though I have fallen, I will stand up;
though I sit in darkness,
the Lord will be my light.

MATTHEW 4:13–16

¹³ He left Nazareth and went to live in Capernaum by the sea, in the region of Zebulun and Naphtali. ¹⁴ This was to fulfill what was spoken through the prophet Isaiah:

¹⁵ Land of Zebulun and land of Naphtali,
along the road by the sea, beyond the Jordan,
Galilee of the Gentiles.
¹⁶ The people who live in darkness
have seen a great light,
and for those living in the land of the shadow of death,
a light has dawned.

Underline the four names in Isaiah 9:6 that describe the ministry and role of Jesus. How does each one invite you to celebrate Him?

DAY 20　　　　　　　　　　　　　　　　　　　　DECEMBER 17, 2021

Illuminated Clay Christmas Trees

ACTIVE TIME
2–3 hours

TOTAL TIME
32 hours

DIFFICULTY
✦ ✦ ✧

These illuminated Christmas trees are a thematic way to decorate your home this Advent season. Display this decoration to remind you of Jesus, the light that pierces through the darkness.

WHAT YOU NEED

2 (8½ x 11-inch) heavyweight cardstock

3 sheets of parchment paper, pre-cut

2 pounds air-dry clay

Rolling pin

Utility knife

Tape

Sponge or cloth

Aspic cutters in desired shapes (We used a star shape)

3 battery-operated LED tea lights

Clay tree templates

 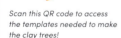

Scan this QR code to access the templates needed to make the clay trees!

WHAT TO DO

Scan the QR code to print the clay tree templates onto 8½ x 11-inch cardstock paper at 100% scale. Cut out the templates and leave them flat.

Place a sheet of parchment paper over the flat template and roll out a ball of clay until it is ⅛ inch thick and large enough to cover the template underneath.

Move the template to place it on top of the clay. Use your utility knife to trace around the template, removing the excess clay. Assemble your paper cone and tape it together so it will be ready to use for the base of your tree.

Lay the paper cone onto the clay shape and wrap the clay around the paper cone. Once it is wrapped around the cone, with your utility knife cut small shallow lines onto the areas where the clay will overlap and wet both cut areas with a sponge or cloth. While supporting the tree from the inside with your other hand, press the two cut edges together and smooth the seam with your wet sponge or cloth.

Press your aspic cutters into the clay while continuing to support from the inside, pressing from the inside with your finger against the cutter. Repeat as desired to create the design wanted. Allow your trees to sit on the cone shape for at least six hours. Then, gently remove the cardstock and let the clay dry out for another twenty-four hours before handling. Place an LED light inside each of your trees. Display in your home throughout the Advent season!

Grace Day

DAY 21

DECEMBER 18, 2021

Advent is a season of celebration and contemplation. We rejoice that our Savior has come to us! We also seek unhurried moments of quiet to reflect on His wondrous light and the promise of His future return. Take time today to pause from the busyness of the season to catch up on your reading, make space for prayer, and rest in God's presence.

For a child will be born for us,
a son will be given to us,
and the government will be on his shoulders.
He will be named
Wonderful Counselor, Mighty God,
Eternal Father, Prince of Peace.

ISAIAH 9:6

DAY 22

A PRAYER FOR

the Fourth Sunday of Advent

The people who live in darkness
have seen a great light,
and for those living in the land of the shadow of death,
a light has dawned.

MATTHEW 4:16

DECEMBER 19, 2021

Light up, O Lord, a brighter and stronger flame in the lamps of Your sanctuary.

Send the arrows of Your quiver deep into our conscience. Clothe Your priests with salvation, that Your saints may shout aloud for joy! Anoint them with Your Holy Spirit, that the aroma of Your grace may spread throughout all Your tabernacles, like fragrant oil poured on the head of Aaron.

Lead us, O Lord, in the way everlasting. Make us resemble our great Master, more and more, as we show grace to others.

Sanctify our hearts by Your grace, that we may be as trees bearing good fruit, or like fountains of pure streams. That is the path to lay up good treasure—it is the way for holiness and compassion to spring forth in freedom, to refresh and give life to everyone around us.

May Your grace animate our souls, Lord. May nothing stand in the way of faithfulness even to death, or deprive us of the crown of life Your grace has promised.

May we receive all those who faithfully proclaim Your word, and welcome them in the name of Jesus. Amen.

PRAYERS OF THE PURITANS

SAINT NICHOLAS

Who was Saint Nicholas?

The real Saint Nicholas was born in the fourth century in what is now modern-day Turkey. He was left with an immense fortune after his parents died early in his life. A devout Christian, Nicholas dedicated his life and his inheritance to caring for the poor and sick. He later became a bishop who was known for defiantly defending church doctrine against Roman orders to renounce Christianity, in spite of persecution and imprisonment.

In one popular legend, Nicholas secretly delivered bags of gold to three young sisters, sneaking the gold into their stockings at night so their impoverished father could use the money for their future dowries. Many people around the world continue to celebrate this legacy of generosity with culturally specific traditions and customs, particularly around giving gifts to children and filling Christmas stockings or shoes.

The Birth of John the Baptist Foretold

23

LUKE 1:5–25

GABRIEL PREDICTS JOHN'S BIRTH

⁵ In the days of King Herod of Judea, there was a priest of Abijah's division named Zechariah. His wife was from the daughters of Aaron, and her name was Elizabeth. ⁶ Both were righteous in God's sight, living without blame according to all the commands and requirements of the Lord. ⁷ But they had no children because Elizabeth could not conceive, and both of them were well along in years.

⁸ When his division was on duty and he was serving as priest before God, ⁹ it happened that he was chosen by lot, according to the custom of the priesthood, to enter the sanctuary of the Lord and burn incense. ¹⁰ At the hour of incense the whole assembly of the people was praying outside. ¹¹ An angel of the Lord appeared to him, standing to the right of the altar of incense. ¹² When Zechariah saw him, he was terrified and overcome with fear. ¹³ But the angel said to him, "Do not be afraid, Zechariah, because your prayer has been heard. Your wife Elizabeth will bear you a son, and you will name him John. ¹⁴ There will be joy and delight for you, and many will rejoice at his birth. ¹⁵ For he will be great in the sight of the Lord and will never drink wine or beer. He will be filled with the Holy Spirit while still in his mother's womb. ¹⁶ He will turn many of the children of Israel to the Lord their God. ¹⁷ And he will go before him in the spirit and power of Elijah, to turn the hearts of fathers to their children, and the disobedient to the understanding of the righteous, to make ready for the Lord a prepared people."

¹⁸ "How can I know this?" Zechariah asked the angel. "For I am an old man, and my wife is well along in years."

¹⁹ The angel answered him, "I am Gabriel, who stands in the presence of God, and I was sent to speak to you and tell you this good news. ²⁰ Now listen. You will become silent and unable to speak until the day these things take place, because you did not believe my words, which will be fulfilled in their proper time."

²¹ Meanwhile, the people were waiting for Zechariah, amazed that he stayed so long in the sanctuary. ²² When he did come out, he could not speak to them. Then

they realized that he had seen a vision in the sanctuary. He was making signs to them and remained speechless. ²³ When the days of his ministry were completed, he went back home.

²⁴ After these days his wife Elizabeth conceived and kept herself in seclusion for five months. She said, ²⁵ "The Lord has done this for me. He has looked with favor in these days to take away my disgrace among the people."

MALACHI 3:1–4

¹ "See, I am going to send my messenger, and he will clear the way before me. Then the Lord you seek will suddenly come to his temple, the Messenger of the covenant you delight in—see, he is coming," says the Lord of Armies. ² But who can endure the day of his coming? And who will be able to stand when he appears? For he will be like a refiner's fire and like launderer's bleach.

> ³ **He will be like a refiner and purifier of silver; he will purify the sons of Levi and refine them like gold and silver.**

Then they will present offerings to the Lord in righteousness. ⁴ And the offerings of Judah and Jerusalem will please the Lord as in days of old and years gone by.

Underline the purpose of John the Baptist's ministry stated in Luke 1:13–17. How does John's purpose change your understanding of Christmas Day?

___

___

___

___

___

___

___

___

___

___

___

___

DAY 23　　　　　　　　　　　　　　　　　　　DECEMBER 20, 2021

HYMN

O Little Town of Bethlehem

Each year She Reads Truth selects the Advent book title from a beloved Christmas hymn. The lyrics of this hymn inspired this year's book title!

WORDS
Phillips Brooks

MUSIC
Lewis H. Redner

An Angel Visits Mary

LUKE 1:26–38

GABRIEL PREDICTS JESUS'S BIRTH

[26] In the sixth month, the angel Gabriel was sent by God to a town in Galilee called Nazareth, [27] to a virgin engaged to a man named Joseph, of the house of David. The virgin's name was Mary. [28] And the angel came to her and said, "Greetings, favored woman! The Lord is with you." [29] But she was deeply troubled by this statement, wondering what kind of greeting this could be. [30] Then the angel told her, "Do not be afraid, Mary, for you have found favor with God. [31] Now listen: You will conceive and give birth to a son, and you will name him Jesus. [32] He will be great and will be called the Son of the Most High, and the Lord God will give him the throne of his father David. [33] He will reign over the house of Jacob forever, and his kingdom will have no end."

[34] Mary asked the angel, "How can this be, since I have not had sexual relations with a man?"

[35] The angel replied to her, "The Holy Spirit will come upon you, and the power of the Most High will overshadow you. Therefore, the holy one to be born will be called the Son of God. [36] And consider your relative Elizabeth—even she has conceived a son in her old age, and this is the sixth month for her who was called childless. [37] For nothing will be impossible with God."

[38] "See, I am the Lord's servant," said Mary. "May it happen to me as you have said." Then the angel left her.

JOB 33:4

The Spirit of God has made me, and the breath of the Almighty gives me life.

FULFILLED IN CHRIST

Luke 1:26–27; Matthew 1:22–23

ISAIAH 7:14

Therefore, the Lord himself will give you a sign: See, the virgin will conceive, have a son, and name him Immanuel.

DANIEL 7:13–14

[13] I continued watching in the night visions,

> and suddenly one like a son of man
> was coming with the clouds of heaven.
> He approached the Ancient of Days
> and was escorted before him.
> [14] He was given dominion
> and glory and a kingdom,
> so that those of every people,
> nation, and language
> should serve him.
> His dominion is an everlasting dominion
> that will not pass away,
> and his kingdom is one
> that will not be destroyed.

Reread Luke 1:26–38 and circle each of the ways Luke's narrative describes Mary's response. How could Mary's anticipation of Jesus inform your own celebration of Jesus's birth?

Rib Eye Roast and Vegetables

PREP TIME
3 days total
6 hours active

COOK TIME
Up to 7 hours and 20 minutes

YIELDS
6–8 servings

DIFFICULTY
★ ★ ★

A note from Chef Simoni:

The method used in this recipe will take time. I recommend starting this process two to three days prior to your dinner to ensure both time for everything else you will need to prepare and plenty of leeway to cook your centerpiece.

INGREDIENTS

RIB EYE ROAST AND SAUCE

5 to 7 pound bone-in rib eye roast or prime rib

2½ tablespoons salt

1 teaspoon black pepper, freshly ground

1 tablespoon olive oil

4 stalks of celery, cut into eight segments each

2 cloves garlic

2 medium onions, quartered

4 large carrots, cut into eight segments each

3 sprigs of rosemary, tied together in bouquet with butcher or kitchen twine

4 to 5 sprigs of thyme, tied together in bouquet with butcher or kitchen twine

2 pounds beef bones or oxtails

1 cup red wine (optional, replace with beef stock)

3 quarts water

5 tablespoons butter

¼ teaspoon salt

1 tablespoon horseradish root, freshly grated

MASHED POTATOES

4 pounds russet potatoes, peeled and quartered

2 cups milk, warmed slightly to 110°F

1½ sticks butter, room temperature

Salt and freshly ground black pepper, to taste

½ tablespoon fresh rosemary, minced (optional)

½ tablespoon fresh thyme, minced (optional)

Chives (optional)

COLLARD GREENS

1 white onion, finely chopped

3 carrots, diced

3 cloves garlic, minced

½ teaspoon turmeric

2 teaspoons canola oil

2 pounds of collard greens, rinsed and cut into 1-inch strips

½ teaspoon cumin

2 tablespoons apple cider vinegar

1 cup beef stock (reserved from the preparation of the rib roast or store-bought)

1½ tablespoons salt

Salt and black pepper, to taste

OPTIONAL ROAST GARNISH

Parsley

Rosemary

Sage

Thyme

Continued

FESTIVE DECORATING TIP

Need a finishing touch for your table this holiday season? Try using linen napkins with natural holiday-themed scents! We used a cinnamon stick and a sprig of winter greenery tied together with cotton twine.

METHOD

3 DAYS BEFORE SERVING

The first step is the selection and preparation of the rib eye roast. As soon as the roast is purchased, season with salt and pepper on a roasting rack that is set inside a pan to give the cut good airflow. Leave uncovered and place in refrigerator.

2 DAYS BEFORE SERVING

Prepare the sauce. Coat a large stock pot with olive oil, then cook the celery, garlic, onions, carrots, rosemary, and thyme for 5 minutes. Add the beef bones and cook for an additional 5 minutes. Add the red wine and water. Simmer for 90 minutes. Strain contents into another large pot and reduce until 4 cups of liquid remain. Reserve the sauce in the refrigerator.

1 DAY BEFORE SERVING

Preheat your oven to 225°F. Take 1 cup of the sauce you've made and place it in the bottom of the roasting pan. Continue to fill the pan with water until there is about ¼ inch of water in the pan.

Next, place the roast, bone side down, on a rack that lifts the roast off the bottom of the pan for proper circulation during cooking. Cook the roast for 4 to 5 hours. Once the roast has reached 128°F internally, you have secured a medium-rare temperature. You can cook the roast 4 to 6 more degrees for a medium level of doneness if you like. Once you've reached the desired level, pull the roast out, and let it rest for 30 minutes, then wrap it in plastic.

Reserve the liquid from the cooking process and add it back to your sauce. Clean out your roasting pan and rack to finish the roast later. In a medium saucepan, bring the sauce to a boil and then let it simmer until it has been reduced by half. Whisk the sauce with butter and salt, off heat. Finish the sauce with fresh grated horseradish, then store in the refrigerator again.

THE DAY OF THE MEAL

Potatoes

Peel and quarter the potatoes and run under cold water in a dutch oven until the water runs clear. Boil the potatoes over medium-high heat until easily pierced with a fork. Drain potatoes, rinse with hot water in a colander, and use a ricer or food mill to strain the potatoes into another pan (or use a hand-masher or stand mixer, if necessary). Add warmed milk and butter to potatoes and season with remaining ingredients to taste.

Collard Greens

In a large dutch oven, sauté onion, carrots, garlic, and turmeric in canola oil. After 3 minutes, add the collard greens in small batches, adding cumin, vinegar, beef stock, and salt after each addition. Cook for 20 minutes. Season with salt and black pepper to taste.

Roast

Remove the roast from the refrigerator 1 hour before reheating. Turn your oven to its highest setting (500 to 550°F). Place the roast in the oven to brown for 5 to 7 minutes.

Remove from the oven and let the roast rest for 10 minutes before cutting. Serve roast uncut on a platter surrounded with parsley, rosemary, sage, and thyme. Once tableside with family or guests, pour a tablespoon or so of the warm sauce over the roast and carve immediately.

DAY 25

An Angel Visits Joseph

MATTHEW 1:18–25

THE NATIVITY OF THE MESSIAH

[18] The birth of Jesus Christ came about this way: After his mother Mary had been engaged to Joseph, it was discovered before they came together that she was pregnant from the Holy Spirit. [19] So her husband, Joseph, being a righteous man, and not wanting to disgrace her publicly, decided to divorce her secretly.

[20] But after he had considered these things, an angel of the Lord appeared to him in a dream, saying, "Joseph, son of David, don't be afraid to take Mary as your wife, because what has been conceived in her is from the Holy Spirit. [21] She will give birth to a son, and you are to name him Jesus, because he will save his people from their sins."

[22] Now all this took place to fulfill what was spoken by the Lord through the prophet:

> [23] See, the virgin will become pregnant
> and give birth to a son,
> and they will name him Immanuel,

which is translated "God is with us."

[24] When Joseph woke up, he did as the Lord's angel had commanded him. He married her [25] but did not have sexual relations with her until she gave birth to a son. And he named him Jesus.

ISAIAH 11:1–9

REIGN OF THE DAVIDIC KING

[1] Then a shoot will grow from the stump of Jesse,
and a branch from his roots will bear fruit.

² **The Spirit of the Lord will rest on him—
a Spirit of wisdom and understanding,
a Spirit of counsel and strength,
a Spirit of knowledge and of the fear of the Lord.**

³ His delight will be in the fear of the Lord.
He will not judge
by what he sees with his eyes,
he will not execute justice
by what he hears with his ears,
⁴ but he will judge the poor righteously
and execute justice for the oppressed of the land.
He will strike the land
with a scepter from his mouth,
and he will kill the wicked
with a command from his lips.
⁵ Righteousness will be a belt around his hips;
faithfulness will be a belt around his waist.

⁶ The wolf will dwell with the lamb,
and the leopard will lie down with the goat.
The calf, the young lion, and the fattened calf will be together,
and a child will lead them.
⁷ The cow and the bear will graze,
their young ones will lie down together,
and the lion will eat straw like cattle.
⁸ An infant will play beside the cobra's pit,
and a toddler will put his hand into a snake's den.
⁹ They will not harm or destroy each other
on my entire holy mountain,
for the land will be as full
of the knowledge of the Lord
as the sea is filled with water.

Underline how the "Spirit of the L{ORD}" is described in Isaiah 11:1–5. How have you seen these characteristics of the Spirit on display this holiday season?

DAY 25

DECEMBER 22, 2021

Mary's Song of Praise

LUKE 1:39–56

MARY'S VISIT TO ELIZABETH

⁣³⁹ In those days Mary set out and hurried to a town in the hill country of Judah ⁣⁴⁰ where she entered Zechariah's house and greeted Elizabeth. ⁣⁴¹ When Elizabeth heard Mary's greeting, the baby leaped inside her, and Elizabeth was filled with the Holy Spirit. ⁣⁴² Then she exclaimed with a loud cry, "Blessed are you among women, and your child will be blessed! ⁣⁴³ How could this happen to me, that the mother of my Lord should come to me? ⁣⁴⁴ For you see, when the sound of your greeting reached my ears, the baby leaped for joy inside me. ⁣⁴⁵ Blessed is she who has believed that the Lord would fulfill what he has spoken to her!"

MARY'S PRAISE

⁣⁴⁶ And Mary said:

> My soul magnifies the Lord,
> ⁣⁴⁷ and my spirit rejoices in God my Savior,
> ⁣⁴⁸ because he has looked with favor
> on the humble condition of his servant.
> Surely, from now on all generations
> will call me blessed,
> ⁣⁴⁹ because the Mighty One
> has done great things for me,
> and his name is holy.
>
> **⁵⁰ His mercy is from generation to generation
> on those who fear him.**
>
> ⁣⁵¹ He has done a mighty deed with his arm;
> he has scattered the proud
> because of the thoughts of their hearts;
> ⁣⁵² he has toppled the mighty from their thrones
> and exalted the lowly.
> ⁣⁵³ He has satisfied the hungry with good things
> and sent the rich away empty.
> ⁣⁵⁴ He has helped his servant Israel,
> remembering his mercy
> ⁣⁵⁵ to Abraham and his descendants forever,
> just as he spoke to our ancestors.

⁣⁵⁶ And Mary stayed with her about three months; then she returned to her home.

PSALM 107:1–16

THANKSGIVING FOR GOD'S DELIVERANCE

⁣¹ Give thanks to the Lord, for he is good;
his faithful love endures forever.
⁣² Let the redeemed of the Lord proclaim
that he has redeemed them from the power of the foe
⁣³ and has gathered them from the lands—
from the east and the west,
from the north and the south.

⁣⁴ Some wandered in the desolate wilderness,
finding no way to a city where they could live.
⁣⁵ They were hungry and thirsty;
their spirits failed within them.
⁣⁶ Then they cried out to the Lord in their trouble;
he rescued them from their distress.

⁷ He led them by the right path
to go to a city where they could live.
⁸ Let them give thanks to the Lord
for his faithful love
and his wondrous works for all humanity.
⁹ For he has satisfied the thirsty
and filled the hungry with good things.

¹⁰ Others sat in darkness and gloom—
prisoners in cruel chains—
¹¹ because they rebelled against God's commands
and despised the counsel of the Most High.
¹² He broke their spirits with hard labor;
they stumbled, and there was no one to help.
¹³ Then they cried out to the Lord in their trouble;
he saved them from their distress.
¹⁴ He brought them out of darkness and gloom
and broke their chains apart.
¹⁵ Let them give thanks to the Lord
for his faithful love
and his wondrous works for all humanity.
¹⁶ For he has broken down the bronze gates
and cut through the iron bars.

Looking back at Luke 1:46–56, underline all of the actions Mary attributes to the Lord, in her life and throughout time. How can your celebration this holiday season reflect God's kindness both in your own life and in redemptive history?

Salted Chocolate Chip Cookies

AND CHOCOLATE SAUCE

PREP TIME
40 minutes

COOK TIME
15–20 minutes

YIELDS
20 cookies with 1½ cups of chocolate sauce

DIFFICULTY
★ ☆ ☆

A note from Chef Simoni:

Cookies are so nostalgic for me, especially during Christmas. In prior kitchens, we would have a special family meal (a meal served to all kitchen and wait staff before a restaurant opens for dinner service). During this time some staff would make cookies for a Christmas cookie swap. One of my dear friends gave this recipe to me and it has been an absolute hit for many years. The chocolate sauce and vanilla ice cream give it the decadence it so richly desires.

INGREDIENTS

COOKIES

1 egg

1 egg yolk

1½ teaspoons sea salt

1¾ cups brown sugar

1 tablespoon vanilla extract

2 sticks unsalted butter, softened

3 cups all purpose flour

1 teaspoon baking soda

2 cups chocolate chips

A pinch of flake sea salt for each ball of dough

CHOCOLATE SAUCE

1¼ cups heavy cream

1 cup chocolate chips

½ teaspoon salt

METHOD

Preheat the oven to 350°F.

Using a stand mixer with the whisk attachment or a hand mixer, mix the egg, egg yolk, salt, ¾ cup brown sugar, and vanilla for 20 minutes on medium speed. The mixture should be pale yellow and hold a ribbon-like pattern when the whisk is pulled from the bowl.

After this process, attach the paddle attachment and beat, on a high speed, the butter and remaining cup of brown sugar for 5 minutes. Turn the mixer down to a low speed and add the flour and baking soda, mixing for about 2 minutes. Add the chocolate chips. Using a rubber spatula, scrape the bowl and make sure the mixture is homogeneous.

Form 1½-ounce (about 1½ inches) balls and place on a cookie sheet. Sprinkle a pinch of flake sea salt on each ball. Bake for 7 minutes, or until golden.

While the cookies are baking, place cream into a medium saucepan over medium heat. After 2 minutes, add chocolate chips and salt. Stir for 5 to 9 minutes until the sauce has a creamy consistency.

Serve warm cookies over a bowl of your favorite vanilla ice cream and drizzle sauce over each portion.

DAY 27

Christmas Eve

The true light that gives light to everyone
was coming into the world.

JOHN 1:9

CHRISTMAS EVE

The Birth of John the Baptist

27

LUKE 1:57–80

THE BIRTH AND NAMING OF JOHN

⁵⁷ Now the time had come for Elizabeth to give birth, and she had a son. ⁵⁸ Then her neighbors and relatives heard that the Lord had shown her his great mercy, and they rejoiced with her.

⁵⁹ When they came to circumcise the child on the eighth day, they were going to name him Zechariah, after his father. ⁶⁰ But his mother responded, "No. He will be called John."

⁶¹ Then they said to her, "None of your relatives has that name." ⁶² So they motioned to his father to find out what he wanted him to be called. ⁶³ He asked for a writing tablet and wrote, "His name is John." And they were all amazed. ⁶⁴ Immediately his mouth was opened and his tongue set free, and he began to speak, praising God. ⁶⁵ Fear came on all those who lived around them, and all these things were being talked about throughout the hill country of Judea. ⁶⁶ All who heard about him took it to heart, saying, "What then will this child become?" For, indeed, the Lord's hand was with him.

ZECHARIAH'S PROPHECY

⁶⁷ Then his father Zechariah was filled with the Holy Spirit and prophesied:

> ⁶⁸ Blessed is the Lord, the God of Israel,
> because he has visited
> and provided redemption for his people.
> ⁶⁹ He has raised up a horn of salvation for us
> in the house of his servant David,
> ⁷⁰ just as he spoke by the mouth
> of his holy prophets in ancient times;

⁷¹ salvation from our enemies
and from the hand of those who hate us.
⁷² He has dealt mercifully with our ancestors
and remembered his holy covenant—
⁷³ the oath that he swore to our father Abraham,
to grant that we,
⁷⁴ having been rescued
from the hand of our enemies,
would serve him without fear
⁷⁵ in holiness and righteousness
in his presence all our days.
⁷⁶ And you, child, will be called
a prophet of the Most High,
for you will go before the Lord
to prepare his ways,
⁷⁷ to give his people knowledge of salvation
through the forgiveness of their sins.
⁷⁸ Because of our God's merciful compassion,
the dawn from on high will visit us
⁷⁹ to shine on those who live in darkness
and the shadow of death,
to guide our feet into the way of peace.

⁸⁰ The child grew up and became strong in spirit, and he was in the wilderness until the day of his public appearance to Israel.

ISAIAH 40:1–5

GOD'S PEOPLE COMFORTED

¹ "Comfort, comfort my people,"
says your God.
² "Speak tenderly to Jerusalem,
and announce to her
that her time of hard service is over,
her iniquity has been pardoned,
and she has received from the Lord's hand
double for all her sins."

³ A voice of one crying out:

Prepare the way of the Lord in the wilderness;
make a straight highway for our God in the desert.
⁴ Every valley will be lifted up,
and every mountain and hill will be leveled;
the uneven ground will become smooth
and the rough places, a plain.
⁵ And the glory of the Lord will appear,
and all humanity together will see it,
for the mouth of the Lord has spoken.

JOHN 1:6–9, 15

⁶ There was a man sent from God whose name was John. ⁷ He came as a witness to testify about the light, so that all might believe through him. ⁸ He was not the light, but he came to testify about the light.

⁹ The true light that gives light to everyone was coming into the world.

…

¹⁵ (John testified concerning him and exclaimed, "This was the one of whom I said, 'The one coming after me ranks ahead of me, because he existed before me.'")

Reflect on how light is present as a comfort in today's Christmas Eve reading. Write a prayer rejoicing that the Light of the World has dawned!

A Prayer for Christmas Day

O God, You have caused this holy night to shine with the brightness of the true Light: Grant that we, who have known the mystery of that Light on earth, may also enjoy Him perfectly in heaven; where with You and the Holy Spirit He lives and reigns, one God, in glory everlasting. Amen.

THE *BOOK OF COMMON PRAYER*

CHRISTMAS DAY

The Nativity

28

LUKE 2:1–20

THE BIRTH OF JESUS

¹ In those days a decree went out from Caesar Augustus that the whole empire should be registered. ² This first registration took place while Quirinius was governing Syria. ³ So everyone went to be registered, each to his own town.

⁴ Joseph also went up from the town of Nazareth in Galilee, to Judea, to the city of David, which is called Bethlehem, because he was of the house and family line of David, ⁵ to be registered along with Mary, who was engaged to him and was pregnant. ⁶ While they were there, the time came for her to give birth. ⁷ Then she gave birth to her firstborn son, and she wrapped him tightly in cloth and laid him in a manger, because there was no guest room available for them.

THE SHEPHERDS AND THE ANGELS

⁸ In the same region, shepherds were staying out in the fields and keeping watch at night over their flock. ⁹ Then an angel of the Lord stood before them, and the glory of the Lord shone around them, and they were terrified. ¹⁰ But the angel said to them, "Don't be afraid, for look,

> **I proclaim to you good news of great joy that will be for all the people:**

FULFILLED IN CHRIST
Jeremiah 23:6

¹¹ Today in the city of David a Savior was born for you, who is the Messiah, the Lord. ¹² This will be the sign for you: You will find a baby wrapped tightly in cloth and lying in a manger."

¹³ Suddenly there was a multitude of the heavenly host with the angel, praising God and saying:

> ¹⁴ Glory to God in the highest heaven,
> and peace on earth to people he favors!

¹⁵ When the angels had left them and returned to heaven, the shepherds said to one another, "Let's go straight to Bethlehem and see what has happened, which the Lord has made known to us."

¹⁶ They hurried off and found both Mary and Joseph, and the baby who was lying in the manger. ¹⁷ After seeing them, they reported the message they were told about this child, ¹⁸ and all who heard it were amazed at what the shepherds said to them. ¹⁹ But Mary was treasuring up all these things in her heart and meditating on them. ²⁰ The shepherds returned, glorifying and praising God for all the things they had seen and heard, which were just as they had been told.

GALATIANS 4:4–5

⁴ When the time came to completion, God sent his Son, born of a woman, born under the law, ⁵ to redeem those under the law, so that we might receive adoption as sons.

CHRISTMAS DAY REFLECTION

Celebrate the birth of Jesus, the Light of the World!
Write a prayer of praise, giving thanks for the gift of
God coming to dwell with us on earth.

DAY 28

DECEMBER 25, 2021

CHRISTMAS DAY SNAPSHOT

Where did I spend Christmas Day?

WHAT TIME DID I WAKE UP?

AM
___
PM

WHAT WAS THE WEATHER LIKE?
(circle one)

° HIGH

° LOW

Who did I celebrate Christmas with?

WHAT MADE ME LAUGH?

WHAT TRADITION MEANT THE MOST TO ME THIS YEAR?

I loved giving:

GIFT

TO

I loved receiving:

GIFT

FROM

HYMN

Hark! the Herald Angels Sing

WORDS
Charles Wesley; altered by George Whitefield

MUSIC
Felix Mendelssohn; arrangement by William H. Cummings

DAY 29

A PRAYER FOR

the First Sunday After Christmas

Because of our God's merciful compassion, the dawn from on high will visit us to shine on those who live in darkness and the shadow of death, to guide our feet into the way of peace.

LUKE 1:78–79

Almighty God, You have poured upon us the new light of Your incarnate Word: Grant that this light, enkindled in our hearts, may shine forth in our lives; through Jesus Christ our Lord, who lives and reigns with You, in the unity of the Holy Spirit, one God, now and for ever. Amen.

THE *BOOK OF COMMON PRAYER*

Jesus Presented in the Temple

LUKE 2:21–40

THE CIRCUMCISION AND PRESENTATION OF JESUS

²¹ When the eight days were completed for his circumcision, he was named Jesus—the name given by the angel before he was conceived. ²² And when the days of their purification according to the law of Moses were finished, they brought him up to Jerusalem to present him to the Lord ²³ (just as it is written in the law of the Lord, Every firstborn male will be dedicated to the Lord) ²⁴ and to offer a sacrifice (according to what is stated in the law of the Lord, a pair of turtledoves or two young pigeons).

SIMEON'S PROPHETIC PRAISE

²⁵ There was a man in Jerusalem whose name was Simeon. This man was righteous and devout, looking forward to Israel's consolation, and the Holy Spirit was on him. ²⁶ It had been revealed to him by the Holy Spirit that he would not see death before he saw the Lord's Messiah. ²⁷ Guided by the Spirit, he entered the temple. When the parents brought in the child Jesus to perform for him what was customary under the law, ²⁸ Simeon took him up in his arms, praised God, and said,

> ²⁹ Now, Master,
> you can dismiss your servant in peace,
> as you promised.
> ³⁰ For my eyes have seen your salvation.
> ³¹ You have prepared it
> in the presence of all peoples—
> ³² a light for revelation to the Gentiles
> and glory to your people Israel.

³³ His father and mother were amazed at what was being said about him. ³⁴ Then Simeon blessed them and told his mother Mary, "Indeed, this child is destined to cause the fall and rise of many in Israel and to be a sign that will be opposed—³⁵ and a sword will pierce your own soul—that the thoughts of many hearts may be revealed."

ANNA'S TESTIMONY

³⁶ There was also a prophetess, Anna, a daughter of Phanuel, of the tribe of Asher. She was well along in years, having lived with her husband seven years after her marriage, ³⁷ and was a widow for eighty-four years. She did not leave the temple, serving God night and day with fasting and prayers.

³⁸ At that very moment, she came up and began to thank God and to speak about him to all who were looking forward to the redemption of Jerusalem.

THE FAMILY'S RETURN TO NAZARETH

³⁹ When they had completed everything according to the law of the Lord, they returned to Galilee, to their own town of Nazareth. ⁴⁰ The boy grew up and became strong, filled with wisdom, and God's grace was on him.

LEVITICUS 12:6–8

⁶ "When her days of purification are complete, whether for a son or daughter, she is to bring to the priest at the entrance to the tent of meeting a year-old male lamb for a burnt offering, and a young pigeon or a turtledove for a sin offering. ⁷ He will present them before the Lord and make atonement on her behalf; she will be clean from her discharge of blood. This is the law for a woman giving birth, whether to a male or female. ⁸ But if she doesn't have sufficient means for a sheep, she may take two turtledoves or two young pigeons, one for a burnt offering and the other for a sin offering. Then the priest will make atonement on her behalf, and she will be clean."

Circle any moments of joy you see in Simeon's and Anna's stories in Luke. In what specific ways have you experienced the joy of Jesus's arrival?

___

DAY 30   DECEMBER 27, 2021

DAY 31

Wise Men Visit the King

MATTHEW 2:1–23

WISE MEN VISIT THE KING

¹ After Jesus was born in Bethlehem of Judea in the days of King Herod, wise men from the east arrived in Jerusalem, ² saying, "Where is he who has been born king of the Jews? For we saw his star at its rising and have come to worship him."

★ **FULFILLED IN CHRIST**
Micah 5:2

³ When King Herod heard this, he was deeply disturbed, and all Jerusalem with him. ⁴ So he assembled all the chief priests and scribes of the people and asked them where the Messiah would be born.

⁵ "In Bethlehem of Judea," they told him, "because this is what was written by the prophet:

⁶ And you, Bethlehem, in the land of Judah,
are by no means least among the rulers of Judah:
Because out of you will come a ruler
who will shepherd my people Israel."

⁷ Then Herod secretly summoned the wise men and asked them the exact time the star appeared. ⁸ He sent them to Bethlehem and said, "Go and search carefully for the child. When you find him, report back to me so that I too can go and worship him."

⁹ After hearing the king, they went on their way. And there it was—the star they had seen at its rising. It led them until it came and stopped above the place where the child was.

¹⁰ When they saw the star, they were overwhelmed with joy.

¹¹ Entering the house, they saw the child with Mary his mother, and falling to their knees, they worshiped him. Then they opened their treasures and presented him with gifts: gold, frankincense, and myrrh. ¹² And being warned in a dream not to go back to Herod, they returned to their own country by another route.

THE FLIGHT INTO EGYPT

FULFILLED IN CHRIST
Hosea 11:1

¹³ After they were gone, an angel of the Lord appeared to Joseph in a dream, saying, "Get up! Take the child and his mother, flee to Egypt, and stay there until I tell you. For Herod is about to search for the child to kill him." ¹⁴ So he got up, took the child and his mother during the night, and escaped to Egypt. ¹⁵ He stayed there until Herod's death, so that what was spoken by the Lord through the prophet might be fulfilled: Out of Egypt I called my Son.

THE MASSACRE OF THE INNOCENTS

FULFILLED IN CHRIST
Jeremiah 31:15

[16] Then Herod, when he realized that he had been outwitted by the wise men, flew into a rage. He gave orders to massacre all the boys in and around Bethlehem who were two years old and under, in keeping with the time he had learned from the wise men. [17] Then what was spoken through Jeremiah the prophet was fulfilled:

[18] A voice was heard in Ramah,

> weeping, and great mourning,
> Rachel weeping for her children;
> and she refused to be consoled,
> because they are no more.

THE RETURN TO NAZARETH

[19] After Herod died, an angel of the Lord appeared in a dream to Joseph in Egypt, [20] saying, "Get up, take the child and his mother, and go to the land of Israel, because those who intended to kill the child are dead." [21] So he got up, took the child and his mother, and entered the land of Israel. [22] But when he heard that Archelaus was ruling over Judea in place of his father Herod, he was afraid to go there. And being warned in a dream, he withdrew to the region of Galilee. [23] Then he went and settled in a town called Nazareth to fulfill what was spoken through the prophets, that he would be called a Nazarene.

JEREMIAH 31:15–17

LAMENT TURNED TO JOY

[15] This is what the Lord says:

> A voice was heard in Ramah,
> a lament with bitter weeping—
> Rachel weeping for her children,
> refusing to be comforted for her children
> because they are no more.

[16] This is what the Lord says:

> Keep your voice from weeping
> and your eyes from tears,
> for the reward for your work will come—
>   this is the Lord's declaration—
> and your children will return from the enemy's land.
> [17] There is hope for your future—
>   this is the Lord's declaration—
> and your children will return to their own territory.

Reread Matthew 2:1–12 and make note of the ways the wise men worshiped Jesus. How have you worshiped Jesus this Advent?

The Journey of the Wise Men

The wise men followed the light of a star to find and worship the newborn King.

No one knows precisely where the wise men came from. Matthew 2:1 tells us only that they came "from the east." Most scholars believe the wise men traveled from Persia through Mesopotamia or from the Arabian peninsula to Jerusalem and then to Bethlehem. This map shows possible routes they may have taken.

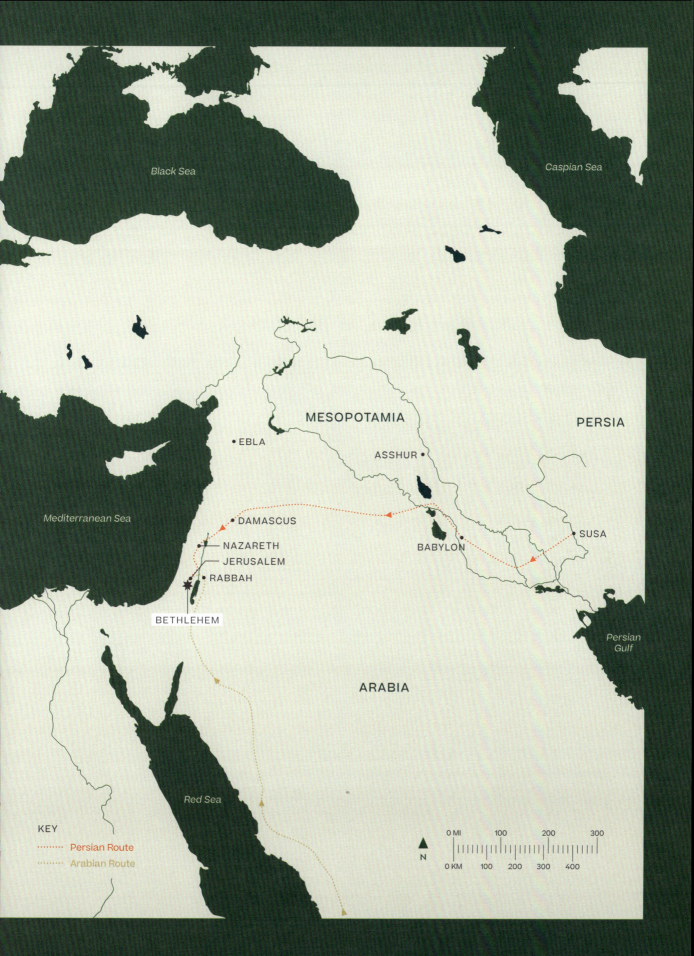

SECTION

4

WAITING FOR THE LIGHT

Night will be no more; people will not need the light of a lamp or the light of the sun, because the Lord God will give them light, and they will reign forever and ever.

REVELATION 22:5

This story didn't begin with a baby in a manger, and it doesn't end there either. Light isn't diminished when we put away the Christmas tree and blow out the last Advent candle. Christmas Day is a celebration of the start of Jesus Christ's life on earth, His ministry, death, and resurrection, and the new life He invites us to enjoy. His work in driving out darkness and making all things new is both already accomplished on the cross and still ongoing.

Until Jesus Christ returns, we share in His work as people of the light, eagerly awaiting that promised day.

DAY 32

The Second Advent

ACTS 1:7–11

⁷ He said to them, "It is not for you to know times or periods that the Father has set by his own authority. ⁸ But you will receive power when the Holy Spirit has come on you, and you will be my witnesses in Jerusalem, in all Judea and Samaria, and to the ends of the earth."

THE ASCENSION

⁹ After he had said this, he was taken up as they were watching, and a cloud took him out of their sight. ¹⁰ While he was going, they were gazing into heaven, and suddenly two men in white clothes stood by them. ¹¹ They said, "Men of Galilee, why do you stand looking up into heaven? This same Jesus, who has been taken from you into heaven, will come in the same way that you have seen him going into heaven."

1 THESSALONIANS 4:16–17

¹⁶ For the Lord himself will descend from heaven with a shout, with the archangel's voice, and with the trumpet of God, and the dead in Christ will rise first. ¹⁷ Then we who are still alive, who are left, will be caught up together with them in the clouds to meet the Lord in the air, and so we will always be with the Lord.

REVELATION 19:6–16

⁶ Then I heard something like the voice of a vast multitude, like the sound of cascading waters, and like the rumbling of loud thunder, saying,

> Hallelujah, because our Lord God, the Almighty,
> reigns!
> ⁷ Let us be glad, rejoice, and give him glory,
> because the marriage of the Lamb has come,
> and his bride has prepared herself.
> ⁸ She was given fine linen to wear, bright and pure.

For the fine linen represents the righteous acts of the saints.

⁹ Then he said to me, "Write: Blessed are those invited to the marriage feast of the Lamb!" He also said to me, "These words of God are true." ¹⁰ Then I fell at his feet to worship him, but he said to me, "Don't do that! I am a fellow servant with you and your brothers and sisters who hold firmly to the testimony of Jesus. Worship God, because the testimony of Jesus is the spirit of prophecy."

THE RIDER ON A WHITE HORSE

¹¹ Then I saw heaven opened, and there was a white horse. Its rider is called Faithful and True, and with justice he judges and makes war.

¹² His eyes were like a fiery flame, and many crowns were on his head. He had a name written that no one knows except himself.

¹³ He wore a robe dipped in blood, and his name is called the Word of God. ¹⁴ The armies that were in heaven followed him on white horses, wearing pure white linen. ¹⁵ A sharp sword came from his mouth, so that he might strike the nations with it. He will rule them with an iron rod. He will also trample the winepress of the fierce anger of God, the Almighty. ¹⁶ And he has a name written on his robe and on his thigh: King of Kings and Lord of Lords.

Where do you see light in today's reading? Pause and reflect on the promise of the second advent, remembering everything you've read in this study.

DAY 32　　　　　　　　　　　　　　　　　　　　　　DECEMBER 29, 2021

The Day Is Near

33

MATTHEW 25:1–13

¹ "At that time the kingdom of heaven will be like ten virgins who took their lamps and went out to meet the groom. ² Five of them were foolish and five were wise. ³ When the foolish took their lamps, they didn't take oil with them; ⁴ but the wise ones took oil in their flasks with their lamps. ⁵ When the groom was delayed, they all became drowsy and fell asleep.

⁶ "In the middle of the night there was a shout: 'Here's the groom! Come out to meet him.'

⁷ "Then all the virgins got up and trimmed their lamps. ⁸ The foolish ones said to the wise ones, 'Give us some of your oil, because our lamps are going out.'

⁹ "The wise ones answered, 'No, there won't be enough for us and for you. Go instead to those who sell oil, and buy some for yourselves.'

¹⁰ "When they had gone to buy some, the groom arrived, and those who were ready went in with him to the wedding banquet, and the door was shut. ¹¹ Later the rest of the virgins also came and said, 'Master, master, open up for us!'

¹² "He replied, 'Truly I tell you, I don't know you!'

¹³ "Therefore be alert, because you don't know either the day or the hour."

DANIEL 2:22

**He reveals the deep and hidden things;
he knows what is in the darkness,
and light dwells with him.**

ROMANS 13:11–14

PUT ON CHRIST

[11] Besides this, since you know the time, it is already the hour for you to wake up from sleep, because now our salvation is nearer than when we first believed. [12] The night is nearly over, and the day is near; so let us discard the deeds of darkness and put on the armor of light. [13] Let us walk with decency, as in the daytime: not in carousing and drunkenness; not in sexual impurity and promiscuity; not in quarreling and jealousy. [14] But put on the Lord Jesus Christ, and make no provision for the flesh to gratify its desires.

1 CORINTHIANS 4:5

So don't judge anything prematurely, before the Lord comes, who will both bring to light what is hidden in darkness and reveal the intentions of the hearts. And then praise will come to each one from God.

1 TIMOTHY 6:12–16

[12] Fight the good fight of the faith. Take hold of eternal life to which you were called and about which you have made a good confession in the presence of many witnesses. [13] In the presence of God, who gives life to all, and of Christ Jesus, who gave a good confession before Pontius Pilate, I charge you [14] to keep this command without fault or failure until the appearing of our Lord Jesus Christ. [15] God will bring this about in his own time. He is the blessed and only Sovereign, the King of kings, and the Lord of lords, [16] who alone is immortal and who lives in unapproachable light, whom no one has seen or can see, to him be honor and eternal power. Amen.

As a follower of Jesus, what does it look like to be light in a dark world? Pause and reflect on the tension of living as light in a world that still chooses darkness.

DAY 33   DECEMBER 30, 2021

HYMN

O Come, O Come, Immanuel

WORDS
Latin hymn; traditional English stanzas 1 and 2 by John Mason Neale; English stanzas 3 and 4 by Henry Sloane Coffin

MUSIC
Plainsong; adapted by Thomas Helmore

DAY 34

The Everlasting Light

ISAIAH 60:19–22

[19] "The sun will no longer be your light by day,
and the brightness of the moon will not shine on you.
The Lord will be your everlasting light,
and your God will be your splendor.
[20] Your sun will no longer set,
and your moon will not fade;
for the Lord will be your everlasting light,
and the days of your sorrow will be over.
[21] All your people will be righteous;
they will possess the land forever;
they are the branch I planted,
the work of my hands,
so that I may be glorified.
[22] The least will become a thousand,
the smallest a mighty nation.
I am the Lord;
I will accomplish it quickly in its time."

REVELATION 21:1–4, 9–11, 22–26

THE NEW CREATION

[1] Then I saw a new heaven and a new earth; for the first heaven and the first earth had passed away, and the sea was no more. [2] I also saw the holy city, the new Jerusalem, coming down out of heaven from God, prepared like a bride adorned for her husband.

[3] Then I heard a loud voice from the throne:

Look, God's dwelling is with humanity, and he will live with them. They will be his peoples, and God himself will be with them and will be their God.

⁴ He will wipe away every tear from their eyes. Death will be no more; grief, crying, and pain will be no more, because the previous things have passed away.

…

THE NEW JERUSALEM

⁹ Then one of the seven angels, who had held the seven bowls filled with the seven last plagues, came and spoke with me: "Come, I will show you the bride, the wife of the Lamb." ¹⁰ He then carried me away in the Spirit to a great, high mountain and showed me the holy city, Jerusalem, coming down out of heaven from God, ¹¹ arrayed with God's glory. Her radiance was like a precious jewel, like a jasper stone, clear as crystal.

…

²² I did not see a temple in it, because the Lord God the Almighty and the Lamb are its temple. ²³ The city does not need the sun or the moon to shine on it, because the glory of God illuminates it, and its lamp is the Lamb. ²⁴ The nations will walk by its light, and the kings of the earth will bring their glory into it. ²⁵ Its gates will never close by day because it will never be night there. ²⁶ They will bring the glory and honor of the nations into it.

REVELATION 22:1–5

THE SOURCE OF LIFE

¹ Then he showed me the river of the water of life, clear as crystal, flowing from the throne of God and of the Lamb ² down the middle of the city's main street. The tree of life was on each side of the river, bearing twelve kinds of fruit, producing its fruit every month. The leaves of the tree are for healing the nations, ³ and there will no longer be any curse. The throne of God and of the Lamb will be in the city, and his servants will worship him. ⁴ They will see his face, and his name will be on their foreheads. ⁵ Night will be no more; people will not need the light of a lamp or the light of the sun, because the Lord God will give them light, and they will reign forever and ever.

What does today's reading say about the everlasting light?

Write a prayer of praise to Jesus,
the everlasting Light of the World.

DAY 34   DECEMBER 31, 2021

Grace Day

DAY 35

JANUARY 1, 2022

Happy New Year! Take time today to pause and reflect on the past five weeks of reading, remembering the promises fulfilled in His first coming and anticipating the promises yet to be fulfilled in His return. Take this first day of the new year to catch up on your reading, make space for prayer, and rest in His presence.

When they saw the star, they were overwhelmed with joy. Entering the house, they saw the child with Mary his mother, and falling to their knees, they worshiped him.

MATTHEW 2:10–11

DAY 36

A PRAYER FOR

the Second Sunday After Christmas

God will bring this about in his own time. He is the blessed and only Sovereign, the King of kings, and the Lord of lords, who alone is immortal and who lives in unapproachable light, whom no one has seen or can see, to him be honor and eternal power. Amen.

1 TIMOTHY 6:15–16

JANUARY 2, 2022

Lord, we commit our souls to Your almighty hand. Under the sanctifying, life-giving, and supporting influences of Your Spirit, help us to wait for Your mercy that leads to eternal life.

Then nothing will sidetrack us—no terror of suffering, allure of pleasure, or false arguments. But guided by the light and truth of Scripture, we will march on to Your holy hill.

And when we escape the dangers of the dark path we are now on, we will greet the dawn of an everlasting day.

Then we will see the Daystar rise, never to set again.
Amen.

PRAYERS OF THE PURITANS

BENEDICTION

Then God said, "Let there be light,"

and there was light.

GENESIS 1:3

FOR THE
Record

How did I celebrate this Advent season?

_____
_____
_____
_____
_____
_____

How did I spend time in contemplation this Advent?

_____
_____
_____
_____
_____

WHAT WAS MY FAVORITE CHRISTMAS CAROL TO SING THIS YEAR?

MY FAVORITE SCRIPTURE FROM THIS ADVENT STUDY:

MY FAVORITE DAY IN THIS ADVENT STUDY:

1	2	3	4	5	6
7	8	9	10	11	12
13	14	15	16	17	18
19	20	21	22	23	24
25	26	27	28	29	30
31	32	33	34	35	36

What does Jesus's declaration that He is the Light of the World mean to me now?

WHAT DID I LEARN THIS ADVENT THAT I WANT TO SHARE WITH SOMEONE ELSE?

What does it look like to reflect the light of Christ in my life and community beyond the holiday season?

HOW WAS CHRISTMAS DAY DIFFERENT THIS YEAR BECAUSE OF WHAT I READ IN THIS STUDY?

In 2021...

How did I see God at work over the past year?

_____

_____

_____

_____

Something God taught me about His character:

Something God taught me about myself:

MY FAVORITE 2021 SHE READS TRUTH STUDY:

AN UNEXPECTED JOY:

AN UNEXPECTED SORROW:

I'm most proud of:

The highlight of my year:

MY PRAYER FOR

2022

___

DON'T STOP READING NOW—START YOUR YEAR IN SCRIPTURE!
Join us for our study of the Gospel of John, starting Monday, January 3.

CSB BOOK ABBREVIATIONS

OLD TESTAMENT

GN Genesis
EX Exodus
LV Leviticus
NM Numbers
DT Deuteronomy
JOS Joshua
JDG Judges
RU Ruth
1SM 1 Samuel
2SM 2 Samuel
1KG 1 Kings
2KG 2 Kings
1CH 1 Chronicles
2CH 2 Chronicles
EZR Ezra
NEH Nehemiah
EST Esther

JB Job
PS Psalms
PR Proverbs
EC Ecclesiastes
SG Song of Solomon
IS Isaiah
JR Jeremiah
LM Lamentations
EZK Ezekiel
DN Daniel
HS Hosea
JL Joel
AM Amos
OB Obadiah
JNH Jonah
MC Micah
NAH Nahum

HAB Habakkuk
ZPH Zephaniah
HG Haggai
ZCH Zechariah
MAL Malachi

NEW TESTAMENT

MT Matthew
MK Mark
LK Luke
JN John
AC Acts
RM Romans
1CO 1 Corinthians
2CO 2 Corinthians
GL Galatians
EPH Ephesians

PHP Philippians
COL Colossians
1TH 1 Thessalonians
2TH 2 Thessalonians
1TM 1 Timothy
2TM 2 Timothy
TI Titus
PHM Philemon
HEB Hebrews
JMS James
1PT 1 Peter
2PT 2 Peter
1JN 1 John
2JN 2 John
3JN 3 John
JD Jude
RV Revelation

BIBLIOGRAPHY

The Book of Common Prayer and Administration of the Sacraments and other Rites and Ceremonies of the Church. New York: Church Publishing, Inc., 1789.

"DIY Porcelain Holiday Tree Lights," A Beautiful Mess, last modified on December 3, 2013, https://abeautifulmess.com/diy-porcelain-holiday-tree-lights/.

Elmer, Robert, ed. *Piercing Heaven: Prayers of the Puritans.* Bellingham: Lexham Press, 2019.

Grant, George and Wilbur, Gregory. *Christmas Spirit: The Joyous Stories, Carols, Feasts, and Traditions of the Season.* Nashville: Cumberland House Publishing, Inc., 1999.

Green, Jonathan. *Christmas Miscellany: Everything You Always Wanted to Know About Christmas.* New York: Skyhorse Publishing, 2009.

Grissom, Fred A. "Church Year." In *Holman Illustrated Bible Dictionary.* Nashville: Holman Bible Publishers, 2003.

Lindsey, Jacquelyn, ed. *Catholic Family Prayer Book.* Huntington: Our Sunday Visitor, 2001.

Mills, Donald. "Light and Darkness," ed. Douglas Mangum et al., In *Lexham Theological Wordbook, Lexham Bible Reference Series.* Bellingham, WA: Lexham Press, 2014.

"Santa Clause," HISTORY, last modified March 10, 2021, https://www.history.com/topics/christmas/santa-claus.

GO DEEPER IN GOD'S WORD NEXT YEAR

Whether you're a seasoned Bible reader or a first-time reader, the She Reads Truth Subscription Box has everything you need to be a woman in the Word of God every day in 2022.

As a Study Book subscriber, we'll do the planning for you! You'll get a brand new Study Book delivered to your door every month, filled with daily Scripture readings and all sorts of extras to help you understand the Bible.

Sign up once and have a plan to stay connected to God's Word on the good days, the bad days, and all the days in between.

USE CODE BOX20 FOR 20% OFF YOUR FIRST MONTH'S BOX

SUBSCRIPTION.SHOPSHEREADSTRUTH.COM

SHE READS TRUTH IS A WORLDWIDE COMMUNITY OF WOMEN WHO READ GOD'S WORD TOGETHER EVERY DAY.

Founded in 2012, She Reads Truth invites women of all ages to engage with Scripture through daily reading plans, online conversation led by a vibrant community of contributors, and offline resources created at the intersection of beauty, goodness, and truth.

As followers of Jesus, we want to know and understand God's Word. But in a world of endless distractions, nonstop notifications, and ever-growing to-do lists, it's easy to feel frustrated or overwhelmed when it comes to reading Scripture.

She Reads Truth exists to equip women to read and know the Bible. Our thoughtfully designed, accessible Bible reading plans and resources—like this one—have helped millions of women worldwide grow in knowledge and affection for God and His Word. All you have to do is show up, read today's scriptures with us, and then do it again tomorrow. It really is that simple.

The Bible isn't just a book. It is living and active, given to us by God so that we can know Him. You are meant to read it. And you can start today.

DOWNLOAD THE APP

VISIT
shereadstruth.com

SHOP
shopshereadstruth.com

CONTACT
hello@shereadstruth.com

CONNECT
@shereadstruth

LISTEN
She Reads Truth podcast

PROUDLY PRINTED IN NASHVILLE, TENNESSEE